Crushes, Flirts, & Friends

Crushes, Flirts, & Friends

A Real Girl's Guide to Boy Smarts

Erika V. Shearin Karres, Ed.D.

Adams Media
Avon, Massachusetts

Published by Adams Media,
an F+W Publications Company
57 Littlefield Street
Avon, MA 02322
www.adamsmedia.com

ISBN: 1-59337-363-5

Printed in The United States of America.

J   I   H   G   F   E   D   C   B   A

Library of Congress Cataloging-in-Publication Data
Karres, Erika V. Shearin.
Crushes, flirts, and friends : a real girl's guide to boy smarts /
By Erika V. Shearin Karres.
p.   cm.
Includes bibliographical references and index.
ISBN 1-59337-363-5 (alk. paper)
1. Teenage girls—Life skills guides—Juvenile literature.
2. Teenage boys—Psychology—Juvenile literature.
3. Interpersonal relations in adolescence—Juvenile literature. I. Title.
HQ798.K352 2005
306.73'0835'2—dc22
2005021912

This book is available at quantity discounts for bulk purchases.
For information, please call 1-800-872-5627.

Dedication

This book is for Elizabeth S. Hounshell and Dr. Mary D. Shearin, my dear daughters, and for Andrew M. Karres, my devoted husband, with all my love and thanks.

Also for June Clark, super agent and mentor.

And for Bridget Brace, a most talented and gifted editor. She knows how to weave raw research material into rad reading material. Thank you so much, Bridget Brace! And for Danielle Chiotti, outstanding editor and earthmover. Not only is Danielle a visionary, but she's also a roll-up-her-sleeves shaker who turns visions into realities. With this book, she helps to empower all the girls in the world to master the relating and dating ABCs *before* they make a huge mistake. So on behalf of girls everywhere now and in the future, thank you, Danielle Chiotti! You're our role and soul model. And for Meredith O'Hayre who always does her best.

Acknowledgments

A very special thanks to all the girls who participated in my research and to my thoughtful teen readers, reviewers, advisers, and real-life experts. And to their parents.

And to Laura O'Brien, an extraordinary educator, and to A.J. Gregory, an inspirational writer. Both Laura and A.J. work hard every day to improve the world.

And to the numerous teachers who offered input and helped gather materials on this most important topic. Now your hard work lives on not only in the academic achievements of your students, but also in the sound decisions and smart life choices your pupils will make.

As a result, you not only touch the future, but also teach and form it.

CONTENTS

Hey There, Girl!

Congratulations to you because you're lucky, smart, and on your way to the top! And you know what? *Now* you're *really* advancing, from this moment on, because you're about to get into the most important topic of your life. And as you do, you'll move straight to the head of your peers and other girls, too. Flat-out zoom right on up there, no matter what your grade was on the last history quiz. And never mind that your homework assignment in Spanish wasn't perfect for once. You rushed through it, but so what? You're not going to worry about that now, because you're into a subject for real life: Boys!

You've already learned to face certain obstacles head-on, be they mean girls or nasty cliques—as you've read in *Mean Chicks, Cliques, and Dirty Tricks*. And with the help of your girlfriends (detailed for you in *Fab Friends and Best Buds*), you can and have overcome obstacles, and you are stronger than ever. But the world of boys will bring you many more obstacles, and a lot of them are hidden like icebergs. Boys can be like a minefield, or a *mind*-field; watch out! Yeah, it's the whole guy world that's so confusing, mind-boggling, and treacherous. Fact is, suddenly you are swimming in this vast ocean of guys. Here a boy, there a boy, everywhere boys! You can't escape them, but you don't want to, actually: You are interested in boys.

> I really, really, <u>really</u> want a boyfriend bad—how can I get one? Tell me the secrets to boys, please. —Angie, 14

Or maybe you don't want much or even anything to do with guys at the moment. You just don't feel ready for the hassles you've heard boys can create.

I don't want a boyfriend. They're nothing but a pain in the butt. Spare me, okay? —Lisa Kim, 14

But you can't avoid boys, no matter how hard you try. And you don't have the slightest idea of how to deal with this whole new world of 'em! Your friends are no help—they are just as clueless as you. How can you tell which boys are second-look worthy and which are not?

The diff between having a nice boyfriend and a bum boyfriend is like the diff between life and death. Trust me. —Cara, 16

Being able to judge boys is crucial. How can you avoid the lurking icebergs, the way deep ditches, the sudden sinkholes? Boys don't come labeled with warning signs. And they sure don't come with an expiration date like peach yogurt does.

Did you know that a lot of boys act so sugar-sweet, but only till you go along with whatever they want, then they drop you like used Kleenex? Be x-tra careful. —Maria Rosa, 15

Fact is, there are wonderful boys—way wonderful ones. But some boys, you need to be extra careful around. This book is going to tell you about the different kinds of boys you'll run into, and whether you should run or stick around.

I need help finding out what boys are good and what are hoods. —Waverly, 14

When you have a problem, you don't just sit there and feel sorry for yourself. No way, you do something! That's why you picked up this book—the girl's guide you need to direct you around the icebergs and the reefs and shallows in the ocean of guys that you find yourself engulfed in. You're going to learn about:

- ✿ The six main types of boys
- ✿ How you can quickly and easily tell the good guys from the bad guys
- ✿ How to avoid those bad guys and meet nothing but the good ones

When you know the secret ins and outs of the guy world, you know it all. —Blair, 15

What you learn *now* about boys will help you for the *rest of your life.*

Why won't anybody tell me the honest truth about boys, boyfriends, and relationships? —Ciella, 14

Don't worry, this book tells the truth, the whole truth, and nothin' but the truth!

Help! I'm on the honor roll in school but flunking the birds and the bees. Not! I know all about that stuff but know <u>nothing</u> about relating and dating. —Hillary, 15

Because more than 1,000 girls and boys revealed their own struggles with relationships and young love, you will have the answers. No identifying information (real names, schools, addresses, or anything else) is given.

If I can spare just one chick from screwing up her life the way I did over some worthless guy, I'll feel better. —Paula, 16

The one thing they all told me was that they wanted to prevent others from making the same mistakes they did.

If somebody had only clued me in about the kinds of guys out there, I wouldn't be crying my heart out now. —Sonya, 16

PART I

Boys 101

Every topic has a special vocab that you learn first. So, of course, there are some words that you need to know before you can get into the ABCs of young love. Before you can really groove to the different kinds of boys, you have to figure out what your feelings *mean*. You want to know the difference between a big crush and a *friend* friend. You want to know the difference between princes (good guys to look for) and frogs (bad boys to watch out for). With other girls helping to define the boy-related terms, we can't lose. Let's get started!

CHAPTER 1

What Do These Feelings Mean, Anyhow?

Crushes ·

Here's the first word: *Crush*. A crush is a feeling you have for someone else. A crush holds the inklings of feelings of love that may develop more deeply down the road. In other words, a crush is usually just a surface thing.

> A crush is a shallow thing—it's liking someone from a big distance, like, someone you don't even know.
> —DeShandra, 14

True, a crush is often something that you suddenly feel about a person glimpsed from afar. You can crush on someone you haven't even met—like a celebrity or the new kid at school. You keep thinking about him 'cause there's just something that caught your eye.

> A crush is going to bed thinking of someone you glimpsed in the hall at school and you just keep thinking about him. You might dream and daydream about him.
> —Sheila, 13

But this obsession with your crush usually fizzles out. Even if the feeling was strong at first, it can ebb off and then go *poof*!

A Crush is a carbonated drink that can lose its fizz. Same with a real crush: It's mainly just temporary. —Courtney, 14

Maybe you feel like a magnet and you're drawn to another person. This can be for lots of reasons—the other person is cute, has a great personality, or just seems cool.

Most often a crush is based on attraction, like the way a guy looks to me. That's all. —Mila, 14

A crush can be minor or major. If it's minor, you just sort of like the person and are glad to see him. If it's a major crush, your heart beats faster when you just hear his name or when you see him way down the hall in school.

Having a crush is liking somebody you don't know well, or not even at all. —Jessica, 14

True. It's the not knowing of that other person that adds to the excitement of the crush. He could be an absolute gem in your head but you'll find out later in the book that sometimes the reality may be very, very different!

Here's my top secret: When I have a crush, the world is way pretty, like all the colors are brighter. —Mason, 15

No matter whether it's a small crush that lasts a few days or a *major* crush that lasts a whole year, crushes are fab experiences to have because they're like baby steps to the real thing—your eventual ability to truly love someone. For that reason, a crush is like phase 1 in your learning all about love and experiencing it firsthand. A crush is fun, it's something to talk about with your fab friends, and it's part of growing up.

Having a crush on a boy in algebra makes the class so much funner. —Morgan, 14

Think of crushes as a baby's crawl stage. Before she learns to walk, she has to learn to crawl. Right? So having a crush is crawling. For a baby, crawling is moving in the right direction—it means she's growing. Same goes for you.

Flirts ·····································

A *flirt* can be a person who flirts—someone who toys with others in a playful, teasing, charming, cute manner. *To flirt* means to act, in some way, on the exciting feeling or the attraction you have for another person. This feeling can come out of a crush, but it doesn't have to. When you decide to flirt, it's because you feel an emotional pull toward someone and you feel you're ready to move on to the next step, which is letting him know you like him.

When you like someone and somehow convey your interest to him, you're the flirter and he is the flirtee. —Simone, 15

Showing that interest can take many forms. People like to flirt in different ways. Maybe you like to touch him on the arm or give him a hug. Maybe you even like to kiss him on the cheek when you flirt. Flirting doesn't have to be way obvious, though. It can happen when you just look at someone longer than usual, and he looks back at you.

Flirting is when you go way out of your way to make eye contact or even make physical contact with a guy. —Darcie, 15

Flirting is a step up from having a crush, because crushes are just feelings without any action. But flirting means you are actually doing something to show how you feel.

Flirting is suggestion through your actions that you are attracted to someone else. But it is just a suggestion. —Lynne, 16

Flirty actions can be as minor as:

✿ Smiling every time you see a boy you like.
✿ Standing near his locker and casually looking over at him.
✿ Waving hi and calling his name.
✿ Talking to him, in a *friend* friend way, a caring way, a gushy mushy way.

No matter what your flirting style is—subtle or not so—flirting takes the attraction you feel and turns it into action. For a baby, it would mean advancing from the crawl stage to the walking stage (with walking and running like being able to love).

Some girls and guys become interested in flirting early. They do this not only because they like someone and want to send a signal, but also because they like flirting just like a hobby, like playing a video game.

Flirting is showing someone you like that you kinda like him. It's like a fun game to me. —Siti, 13

And some girls get into flirting later . . .

I never thought about flirting but once I tried it, I liked it. Nothing to it—just act like you're interested in a boy and, like, smile and nod a lot. —Abigail, 15

And still other girls actually develop special skills at flirting since they do it a lot . . .

My top flirting secret is to touch my hair in a way that says, "See how I'm touching my hair? I wouldn't mind if you touched my hair this way." Works for me. —Audrey, 16

Still other girls come up with their own top routines . . .

Another way to flirt is to cuddle yourself, like, you nuzzle your cheek next to your shoulder and bat your eyelashes. —Charlize, 16

Yet another group of flirters sticks with the golden oldies . . .

The art of flirting has been expanded over the years but I suggest the greats—tracing the ground with the tip of your shoe and blushing. Act like this guy is sooo great you're, like, way overcome. —Jeena, 15

Sometimes the action or the words in flirtation are *sincere*. Other times, they're not—they're planned, pretend types of gestures or prerehearsed words that are used every time. So being careful is a must—whether you're doing the flirting or are the receiver of the flirting. Remember, flirting isn't just done by girls; boys get into it too.

Once you know the flirting basics, flirting is harmless—unless you go overboard. Then it's dangerous because it can send the wrong signals.

Here's my top flirting advice: Never act like you're Britney Spears in an MTV video. Be true to yourself, to your best self. —Ann, 16

Yeah, flirting that's gross, that crosses the line and doesn't hold back some, can actually hurt you and your rep. For one thing, it makes a girl look less than her best. It takes away from her value, her self-esteem. Inside, she feels bad when she flirts all-out. Plus, guys might not realize that she's only playing, which is what flirting means—to tease and play with someone. Over-the-top flirting

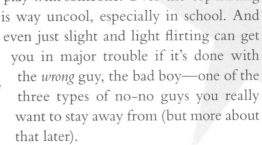

is way uncool, especially in school. And even just slight and light flirting can get you in major trouble if it's done with the *wrong* guy, the bad boy—one of the three types of no-no guys you really want to stay away from (but more about that later).

Friend Friends· · · · · · · · · · · · · · · · · · · ·

After the flirting comes feeling *more* for someone. After you flirted with him and he flirted back, your feelings for him became stronger and more meaningful. You both tell each other that you really like one another, and you call him your *friend* friend or your boyfriend.

> When I was a freshman, I started liking this guy that I thought was the most wonderful person I'd ever met, and he liked me too. So we became boyfriend/girlfriend. —Amy Kim, 15

Best of all, when you have a Prince boyfriend, he's not afraid to show it with words and actions. He lets other boys know, too, that he has feelings for you.

So, comparing this to the baby again, that would mean she's walking well now—not dancing or playing ball yet, but able to make it across the room quickly, on two feet and staying upright.

> Having a boyfriend is like not having to talk all the time when you hang out. It's just being comfortable together. —Patsy, 16

And here's more knowledge for you, girl: For a boy to be your *friend* friend, it means he's a person who you have a crush on, and you let him know about your crush by flirting with him. Next, you feel you like him in a more serious way—like you could, if things work out someday, even have a closer relationship with him (hello, boyfriend!).

> How can you tell if he's, like, your <u>friend</u> friend? Maybe when his friends become your friends, and yours become his. —Carlie, 16

While crushing is one-sided and often spur-of-the-moment, and flirting is acting romantic in a playful, teasing manner, having a *friend* friend is more serious and *two-sided*.

Unfortunately, having the wrong boyfriend can really, really get you into trouble. It can make you feel like your life is rocketing downhill with no end in sight.

This bad guy almost drove me into a bottomless black hole.
—Mia, 15

Once you learn what to look out for, you will avoid those boys who could really mess things up for you. Keep reading!

CHAPTER 2

Frogs and Princes, and Some Rules to Read By

In this book, a *Prince* is a boy with good qualities that you admire. A Prince is a boy you can like if you want to, and everyone will agree with you that this boy is worthy of your time. Of course, a Prince isn't perfect—who is?—but he's a boy with at least a few princely qualities. That means he's nice and polite, smart and respectable, and he looks good—to you, anyway.

A *Frog* is the opposite of a Prince. Any boy who has qualities that make him a bad choice for you is a Frog. That doesn't mean he's a terrible boy or a hopeless-forever boy or a worthless creature. Just like in the fairy tale, a Frog has come to mean any guy who isn't the best for you or who doesn't measure up to your standards. (Of course, there could be a whole other book on why calling some boys Frogs is doing them—and frogs—an injustice.) So a Frog, in this book, is a guy you don't want to be around too much. And you surely don't want to have a crush on him—unless you're planning to go into pond and swamp biology as a career.

This one boy I was always having to hide from my 'rents. Please tell me how to find one I can, like, show off. —Suzie, 14

For sure, a Prince isn't someone you have to sneak past your folks, or who makes you feel yucky or gives you a creepy feeling. Actually, a Prince is in the guy world what you are in the girl world—a Princess!—and someone on the way up, someone who's trying to reach his potential.

Cool Rules· ·

With all the way cool boys out there, what if you don't recognize them because you don't know what to look for? Or, what if you have a chance to pick a perfect Prince and you end up with a yucky Frog instead?

What if, by chance, I only get to meet up with the wrong guys—the uncool dudes, the duds? HELP! —Ashlee, 15

That would be awful, Ashlee. But you have a point. What a crying shame that would be—to have so much opportunity right at your fingertips and let it (him) all slip away. Don't worry—we won't let that happen!

As you read this book, keep in mind these two basic rules:

1. You want the hard facts—which boys are hot and which are not, so the info you get will be in categories. Please never use any term you read here as a name-calling excuse. Please don't ever say to a new boy you meet, "Hey, you're a So-and-So. Says right here on page seventy-eight." That would be so not hot, to try and lay a guy low and hurt him. And it's the exact opposite of the purpose of this book. The purpose of this book is to teach you to first look, understand, and classify. And then, armed with reams of relationship knowledge, you can decide which of the cool dudes are the ones you might possibly be interested in, and which guys are lacking, so you can send them packing.

2. This book isn't just for girls, although it's written for girls most of all. So anybody, yes, even parents, teachers, and *boys* included, is invited to get in on the top secrets of real live girls and guys.

PART II

The Bonus Boys: The Princes

Good news, girl! The nice boys in your life outnumber the not-nice ones by far. Not all of the good guys are super Princes, but they're who you want to start with in matters of your heart. As you delve into their behaviors and attitudes, you will learn how to spot them and how to "not" them. They are presented in Part II in ascending order—from plain nice, to nicer, to super-mega nice. Let's start meeting them!

CHAPTER 3

The Geek, aka the Brainiac or the Striver

The Geek is a boy who, at first glance, may not look like anything special. But overall, he's a good guy and someone you really ought to take a closer look at. He has his ups and downs for sure, but mostly he's pleased with his life, or most aspects of it. He doesn't necessarily love all his classes or his whole schedule, but he enjoys most school things and teen challenges. So, you'll find the Geek in a good mood most days. Sure, he can goof off majorly, but only when it's warranted.

BOY WATCH: What Makes a Boy a Geek?

Jeff gets to school just as the first bell rings. He races up to the photo lab on the second floor, where he's supposed to drop off a picture he snapped at the last football game. No prob there, except Jeff has to hustle to get the job done before the second bell. He was up late, messing around with his phone and PC last night, so he overslept and didn't have time to pick out a cool outfit. He just threw something on—an old T-shirt and his usual jeans and flip-flops. As he crosses the school lobby, he's got a faraway look on his face 'cause he's wondering if this football pic should go flush right or flush left on the fourth page of the school paper, or if it should appear in the middle of the text. He almost runs you over!

"That rude dude," you think, but you know he isn't really. Later, when you see him between first and second periods, he actually says, "Sorry. Didn't mean to bump into you." You mutter, "No problem," and maybe you even smile, a little.

You just met the first type of Prince: the Geek.

Dear Dr. Erika:
There's this guy in my English class who isn't really that hot: Brown hair, sorta skinny, three medium-sized acne scars that are actually kind of cute. Last week, when my teacher talked about alliteration and everybody was sooo bored, he raised his hand and said, "What about the 'hallowed halls of Hudson High'?" I thought this was cool, so now I'm paying more attention to him.

Martie, 15

Dear Dr. Erika:
Whenever I think of myself and this certain boy—he's in my trig class and is really smart but not a show-off—I get all fluttery inside. He's just a quiet guy who nobody makes a fuss over, but he knows his work and cares about his grades. Plus, he's into chess and all kinds of brain games. Anyway, I, like, visualize a radiant mermaid resting upon rocks in the ocean, and the waves playing with her hair. And then (this is so embarrassing) I think of a shipwrecked fisherman showing up and he has the face of that brainy guy I like!

LaKiara, 14

F Y I

The Geek is a nice boy who looks unpolished but has lots of potential. Usually he's the kind of boy who's a whiz in at least one area. He may not be well rounded, and he often doesn't have the best manners or the smoothest style—yet.

He can come across as awkward and absentminded, but he's always well mannered. He might be preoccupied and take the up staircase for walking downstairs—a no-no at your school—but when someone reminds him, he's not belligerent and he mumbles a sorry.

The Geek might wear clothes out of season—a flannel shirt in summer, a sporty T-shirt in winter. He may even wear the same jeans a bunch of times during the week. But he's not dirty! New clothes just aren't on his radar screen. He may carry almost nothing to class and have to borrow paper and a pencil from you, or he carries a stack of tech stuff and several calculators.

He may be the kid in class who the teacher frowns over now and then. Or he can be the one everyone calls the teacher's pet. The one thing is that the Geek always, always does have at least *one* passion. Like you have that fashion passion, he is into engineering or architecture or creating his own new and hot recipes.

The Geek usually knows already in middle school what he's into, and if that something is taught in school, he excels in it. If his "thing" isn't taught at school, he saves his energy and creative drive for after-school activities or clubs. Some people call this energy and drive *juice*. Well, the Geek's got it. He's active and on the go, and even when he chills, his brain's never still.

Some Geeks also love individual sports, like cross-country, golf, diving, or archery—anything wherein they can mostly compete with themselves. Sometimes, they start their own sports club, like for playing Hacky Sack or Frisbee.

Usually, I form crushes on the top hotties, but there have been a few cases when I was attracted to guys who other girls aren't even interested in. And they were always the best—super nice and way reliable. —Brit, 16

Above all, the Geek isn't after popularity. He's just trying to find himself and make it through middle and high school the best way he can, without too much of a hassle. And the good news is, he gets a kick out of learning something new and different, although it's not always on the teacher's lesson plan. He for sure doesn't always do things right, but he'll come around.

In short, the Geek can be the driving force behind any bunch of guys; he can be hilarious and bright. He can also be sort of a low-key, stand-aside guy with just a few friends.

A Geek sometimes likes to be left alone so he can do his thing. That doesn't mean he shuns pals. He may just need a nudge now and then to join up with the crowd.

He's not pushy; he's pretty much set and on the right track. And he's glad to help others—girls and guys—move ahead and get on the right track too. You've just got to get to know him.

Universal High School

Deanne's first project as a student government rep was to help organize a back-to-school dance to which the other high schools in her area were also invited. Deanne suggested a theme and helped put up the bright streamers on the day of the dance. Then, she ran home and changed from her school uniform to a pair of dressy slacks and a girly top, fixed her hair special, and headed back to the gym.

She looked around to find her friends and spotted them across the room, dancing in a huge circle. When she got closer, she saw an unusual guy—not cute, but different looking. He had dirty-blond, kinda shaggy hair; ocean-blue eyes that squinted behind tiny glasses; and a way lopsided smile.

Long story short, this "stranger" was actually in Deanne's economics class—his name was Eddie and he sat in the back while she sat in the front. After the dance, every day Deanne would smile at Eddie when she entered the economics room and he always smiled back.

A month later, out of the blue, Eddie fell into step with Deanne as she left the room, and he walked her to her next class. They laughed about their econ teacher, "Mr. Volcano," and Eddie asked her why she didn't bring an umbrella. Mr. Volcano got so excited when he taught that he actually spit all over the front row! A week later, Eddie asked her for her phone number. When they talked on the phone, he didn't have much to say and she didn't have much to say either. Eventually, Deanne started going to watch Eddie's tennis matches and cheered for him even though he lost. Notes, flowers, and double dates with Deanne's best friend followed. Eddie proved to be sweet plus smart. He knew answers to many of Deanne's questions about school stuff; he also encouraged her to think deeply about a lot of things. She could act silly and he never once told her she was dumb. On the contrary, he told her she was smart and pretty.

Eventually, Eddie won a tennis match by the end of the year, and Deanne made nothing lower than a B− for the first time in her life! Plus she had tons of fun, having found her Princely Geek among all the Frogs.

Could You Be a Geek Repellent?

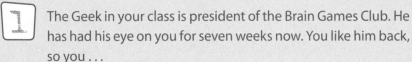

1 The Geek in your class is president of the Brain Games Club. He has had his eye on you for seven weeks now. You like him back, so you . . .

- **a.** Do nothing. You hope he'll say "hello" before the semester ends, or maybe before next year.
- **b.** Make it a point to give him more chances to have his eyes on you. You trail him to his locker, walk slowly past the classroom where his club meets, and sit sideways in your desk so he can see your hot profile.
- **c.** Make him your next conquest, stat. You're the Tom Hanks to his Leo in *Catch Me If You Can*. You're hot on the trail and will not fail.

d. Start slow and work your way up. You ask his advice on what flick to see with your buds. If he invites himself along, great! If not, maybe he will next time, no sweat.

2 For the past three weeks, you can't get that quiet, smart kid from chem class off your mind. Whenever you hear a love song, you suddenly start thinking of him again. Finally, you . . .

a. Write a poem about him in your diary and doodle his name during class. You keep your eyes locked on your notebook, terrified he might catch you staring at him one day.

b. Sit next to him one day and drop your pen on the floor so he has to pick it up. When he does, you say "Thank you," but don't meet his eyes.

c. Do everything in your power to get him to fall head over heels in love with you—fast. You wear your mini-est skirt and cutest top. That's sure to open his eyes wide!

d. Ask him to be in your group for group assignments. It's clear that he knows his schoolwork, and hopefully you and your new friend will learn from each other.

3 The star in your math class has recently acted really playful toward you. He hides your book, draws on your paper, and moves his chair over to you from across the room when the teacher calls for group work. You . . .

a. Run to Guidance and ask for another schedule. You don't want to be in class with a boy who singles you out to embarrass you. You're outta there.

b. Blush, flush, and gush a lot. You flutter your eyelashes as you move your chair away from him but ever so slowly, so everybody notices. Isn't it nice to get all this attention?

c. Match him move for move, then up his gestures. He hides your book, so you hide his backpack. He draws on your paper, so you draw on his shirt.

d. Tell your friends to tell his friends that this overfussing about you makes you feel uncomfortable. If he has a crush on you, he'll shape up and you can at least be friends.

 You like a new, behind-the-scenes smart guy who is highly respected by everyone—even the tough swim coach. But the new boy doesn't seem to like you that way. You . . .

a. Develop a substitute crush on a movie star who resembles your unrequited crush.

b. Ask your friends to keep their ears open to any gossip that's going around. While your friends gather all the info they can, you wring your hands and wait, wonder, and worry.

c. Join the swim team even though your butterfly stroke is more like the housefly stroke. But hey, with that teeny bikini you wear whenever you have free swim, your hottie won't be able to take his eyes off you.

d. Start a short conversation with him. This Geek's got potential, in your opinion, but he's just one of so many nice guys you could be interested in.

> Now it's time to find out your true Crush Quotient, your CQ. Tally your answers and find the description that best fits you. If you have a mixture, look at all the breakdowns. Obviously, there's a bit of everything in you, which is fab. Now, can you work on having a little less of the answer A attitude and a little more of the answer D attitude?

Mostly A's: Pining Penelope

It's great to know how sensitive you are, the deep feelings you have, and how much you're into romance. You're the one who still has all the Valentines from second grade, aren't you? But you don't want to be a wallflower all your life. Why don't you take a deep breath and get over the scaries.

Boys are people, just like girls. Until you actually meet one or two or three up close, how can you know what they're made of?

Mostly B's: Nail-Biting Norma

It's normal to be nervous around guys, especially ones you like. And congrats to you for overcoming your nervousness and trying to show the guys you're ready to transition from daydreaming to being a dream girl. Develop more confidence and always know boys are just a small part of your life, not your whole entire life.

Mostly C's: Colleen the Conqueror

You don't have to tackle boys like they're the enemy! Slow down and think about your goals. Back off and relax. You don't have to drag every halfway hottie off to your cave.

Mostly D's: Top-of-the-World Tina

You're handling the boy scene just fine! You are friendly, but not too friendly. You are giving your crush and even noncrushes the chance to get to know you, but you're not chasing after them as if your life depended on them. You're on your way to your own best life.

GEEK FACTORS: What Should You Know about the Geek?

First off, you should realize there are lots of Geeks out there, and they are all uniquely different. They make up the majority of the good guys in most schools, and they come in all shapes and sizes. They may not knock you over at first glance, but they're prizes.

> My sister had this huge crush on an average-looking guy. Everyone made fun of her. The other girls said he wasn't cute enough, but after a while, they had to admit that he was super nice. —Dalton, 15

A Geek is a boy you can have a solid friendship with in addition to having a crush on him. You can be extra comfortable with him because he is interested in a class you like or a subject you're into, so there's always something that bonds you. Maybe it's just history homework, but it works as a starting point.

Although most of them are Princes, Geeks can sometimes not be straightforward with their feelings. You may think the Geek sees you just as a gal pal, but he has more in mind. All you have to do is speak up and ask.

GEEK SIZZLERS:
What You Should Do about the Geek

Underneath his rumply, frumpy appearance, the Geek has goals. He makes plans for himself—some are realistic and others are off the wall. But that means he likes girls who have something going on besides worrying about their latest pedi or mani all the time.

> Talking or texting lots with a Geeky guy is usually considered a good thing—as long as the target is attention-worthy. And he is, if he's smart in something. —Mattie, 15

To keep the Geek talking, get busy and research something he seems to be into. That way, you'll know a thing or two when he holds forth about his fave topics. Maybe you can even hit him over his tousled head with a few facts he's overlooked. You should also be up on the latest, greatest alternative or rock bands and tunes if that's your style, because the Geek loves different kinds of music.

> If you're into the bands and music a Geek likes, he may not be able to resist you. That little crush may accelerate very quickly into something else. —Lisa, 16.

Even more importantly, develop your own passion for something. Geeks like to have good, long conversations about all kinds of things besides ringtones. Go on, get on the Internet highway and explore.

The Geeks I know don't feed you the smoothest lines, but they've really good listeners. So you better have something to dish on besides the hottest nail polish. —Neville, 15

BOY STORY—A Real-Life Story from a Girl Like You

Many people say that high school love is just puppy love and that it won't last. In most cases, this is true, but then there are always those few couples that go off to school but stay together and marry young.

Ted was in my computer club; that's how we met. He was always busy with his Web site and putting together the school's e-zine. He's two years older than me but we've managed to stay together even though I am still home and he's in college on the other side of the country. Of course, I still have these images in my head of my wedding day and walking down the aisle with Ted. But then reality kicks in and I remind myself that I am only seventeen years old and haven't even graduated yet! Ted's physical distance off at school has kind of put a distance into our relationship. He doesn't call as much and isn't as thoughtful. But it's OK. Ted has to walk his walk. Meanwhile, I just try to be strong and not make any waves for him. I focus on myself so I can grow up into the best girl I can be. That's my #1 job right now—focusing on ME!

Lexi, 17

O H B O Y – M E T E R

Grade the Girls

A+ for you, Lexi. Good job! To be strong and concentrate on your own growth really is your #1 job right now. Sure, it's nice to hold on to your best Geek friend. But being a Geek means he's a guy in the process of growing up too. He's not done yet. He might follow a growth pattern that meshes with yours, or one that's his very own. He's away at college, changing and meeting new people. Instead of latching on to him in a clingy way, you're doing the mature thing. You wish him well and concentrate on yourself. Bravo!

PRINCESS PROMOTERS: Time for Some Add-Justments

What's so super great is that you can change the type of guys you meet by changing yourself just a little. By making a little positive adjustment here or there, you will improve your chances of meeting nothing but Princes. The changes you can make are actually add-justments. That means, all you have to do is add a little something to what you're already doing. It's like adding a + sign to yourself!

> To find a really cool dude, you gotta be a really terrific chick. That means, like, never stop working on yourself. Make yourself all you can be. Work on it hard but not for him. Do it for yourself! —Ayla, 17

1. The first add-justment to make is in your attitude. It's a fact that being positive makes everything in your life go better. So add a smile to your nonsmiley times. Three times a week, when you feel down in the dumps, smile.
2. Think more positive thoughts. Three times this week, when things don't go your way, say to yourself, "Hey, coulda been worse." The nail you broke was just on one finger. The bad

hair day was only on Tuesday, not all week. That strikeout wasn't a big deal because you'll hit a home run in the next game. See, how easy it is to turn things around?

3. Pay three compliments every week to girls who least expect them. Find something special about girls you usually don't chat with and tell them. Start noticing the positives in your group, not just among the inner, but also the outer loop. In this way, you'll add to yourself by adding a little sunshine to other people's lives.

Boy Secrets

How do the Geeks in your world react to girls who have caught their eye? Some Geeks are way shy. They want to get to know you but don't know how to do it. So they pretend they don't care about a girl, or sometimes they even say something a little mean.

> When I like a girl, I don't know what comes into me, but first thing I do is try to hide my feelings way deep down. —Tim, 15

It depends on the girl if this approach works or not. Many Geeks would like to start talking to girls but are afraid to say the wrong words.

> I don't do anything, just look and wait around for a girl to give me a smile, or a hint of a wink, or some little sign—something. —Jim, 16

Other Geeks realize that maybe they aren't the hottest dressers or the coolest dudes. They're not Mr. Popularity or gossiped about a lot, so they quietly try hard to make a good impression.

> When I see a girl I like, I try to act in a manner in which I can show off my best side. I'm extra polite, even to the teachers. —Ryan, 17

And some Geeks suddenly start changing their looks—or try to at least, on mornings when they're not too rushed. Some actually comb their hair or wear a different T-shirt, for a change.

When I'm interested in a girl, I spend more time fixing my hair, wearing my better stuff, standing up when she's around, you know. Stuff like that. —Mike, 15

(How different from the next type of nice boy who wears nothing but his best all the time!)

Boy File

To do this fun activity for each type of boy, you're going to need a stack of 3×5 note cards and a box to put them in. (You know, the kind of metal or plastic box that's used to file recipes or term-paper notes.) This is going to be your new Boy File! You can vent on these cards and let out all your feelings about boys. Take the first few cards and write at the top of each: GEEKS. Then, write down the names of any boys you know who fit that category, and why they fit. Fill in each Geek's one or two talents or major interests. If nothing comes to your mind, just leave a blank for the time being. Next time you're near this Geek, take a closer peek at him.

On your Geek cards, write down why you are curious about each one. You can also write down anything that comes to your mind about boys in general. If you want, you can even use your Boy File cards as a top points collection only, and use an old notebook for longer rants and raves.

Crush Code

Only one rule to follow with your Boy File: Use the Crush Code. That means, whenever you write down the name of a *real* boy, use only his initials and reverse them. For example, if the boy's name is Dan Richardson, and his initials are D. R., you should reverse his initials and refer to him as "R. D." Get creative and add a letter of your choice in the middle—for instance, adding an *E* makes the word *RED*, as in *red hot*. Have fun with your Crush Code, and be sure to keep referring to this particular Geek by his Crush Code name: *Red*.

Use your guy file to store and collect your thoughts on all the boys at your school. When you head off to school, just take a few blank cards, snap a rubber band around them, stick them in your backpack, and you're good to go. Be sure not to leave them lying around at school, and share them with only fab friends you really trust. If you stop crushing on a guy, just remove him from the Boy File!

Final Exam

Someday you'll probably take a class or a test or a quiz that is graded as pass/fail—P or F. We need a system to rate the types of guys in your life, but our P/F system isn't based on pass/fail. It's a Prince/Frog system. Anytime we give a boy a P, it means he's tending toward Princely behavior. And anytime we give him an F that means he's not so hot and leaning toward the Froggie side of things, and that's bad.

This rating system's way easy to learn. Bet you'll be pulling out your Boy File and rating away!

This report card breakdown gives you an overview of each boy and all the things he does. It determines if he's crush worthy, which may lead to flirt worthy, or even boyfriend worthy. There are five basic categories by which you should judge each boy. They are:

1. Looks, **2.** Schoolwork, **3.** Attitude, **4.** Behavior, **5.** Activities/sports

And the final score can be:

→ **Pitiful**—a real Frog (4 or 5 F's)
→ **Poor**—a Frog (3 F's)
→ **Possible**—has Prince possibilities (2 F's)
→ **Powerful**—a Prince in the making (1 F)
→ **Perfect for you**—a true Prince (0 F's)

So what does the Geek score on his final?

The Geek's Report Card

Looks: F, though not always, and certainly not in your opinion!
Schoolwork: P, though not in every subject
Attitude: P
Behavior: P
Activities/sports: F or P, it depends

Added up, that means the Geek gets 1 or 2 F's. That puts his Prince-for-you potential between possible and powerful. Check out the Geeks in your life—they have potential!

CHAPTER 4

The Go-Getter

You know the Go-getter; he's into lots of things at school, at home, in the community, in his place of worship—and he's *loving* it. The Go-getters make up a huge section of the nice guys at your school. They're impressive and likable and fun to know 'cause most every Go-getter is so evenly balanced and well rounded.

> There's this group of boys in my school who, like, run everything, and they really get stuff done.
> —Loris, 13

Yes, those are the Go-getters! They're good in a lot of things and they like to try a bunch of activities. Often they're the athletes who aren't necessarily starters on the varsity team, but they try. Even on the bench, they keep morale high for their teams.

> The nicest guys in my school are the ones who are, like, team players—not the top dogs but part of the pack.
> —Emelia, 14

Go-getters have tons of school spirit and drive, and they still keep their grades up and do their homework. They're called the Go-getters because they're on the go and they're the go-to guys, the ones other kids turn to. And they don't let you down.

BOY WATCH:
What Makes a Boy a Go-Getter?

You can always tell when Justin's nearby. Before he even comes down the hall and enters the cafeteria, you can hear the laughter—his and his buds'. Usually he's got three, four, or five other guys orbiting around him like satellites or walking in a row. And when they've found their fave hangout spot, a few more guys and some girls crowd around. They talk Red Sox and Yankees—whom they call the Tankies, after the 2004 fiasco. Or they talk about NASCAR or Formula 1 racing, or video games.

The topic of the convo is usually something guy-related but not real serious, except when it's about Justin's own team and the State Conference. Today, Justin talks about the chances of the jayvees from his school beating a neighboring school's team. The girls join in by trotting out facts about the teams. Someone reminds Justin of his own performance at the last game. It sure wasn't scout-worthy. And what does he do? He just laughs and says, "So what? I'm gonna do better next time." With his playing a couple of different sports, running the Movie Club, and being at the top of the class, you know that Justin is definitely a Go-getter.

Dear Dr. Erika:

Oh man, I'm so in love with the most fab boy at my school, but so are about umpteen other chicks who're way prettier and smarter than me. So I just try to out-admire those chicks by hanging around this boy nonstop and telling him how super great he is. And when he wants something, like from the snack machine, I fly over there and get the chips for him before any of the other girls can. He always wolfs them down, then turns his back on me and talks to these other chicks. But when those other girls are in class or have a meeting, he's like, "Oh, hi," to me—like he's sooo glad to see me. What's the deal?

Bonnie, 14

```
Dear Dr. Erika:
    My best friend, DeeDee, has a boyfriend that I like a
    lot. He's cool and has lots going for himself. He's in
    the eighth-grade talent show, plays baseball, and gets
    to make the morning announcements over the intercom!
    Wow. Now DeeDee says she's tired of him and wants to
    just be good friends with him. Meanwhile, I'm dying
    to get to know him better. It's getting so I wake up
    nights thinking about him! What should I do?
                                                   Robin, 13
```

Sounds as if both Bonnie and Robin are dealing with the Go-getter. Bonnie won't find her Go-getter liking her any better as long as she pays so much attention to him. She needs to focus on *herself*! Robin needs to talk to DeeDee before she can do anything about her Go-getter. Usually even your fab friends won't be cool with you flirting with or crushing on their ex.

F Y I

The Go-getter is a boy who's popular with a lot of students, teachers, and parents. That's because he's got a good personality and isn't lazy (except when he's supposed to read *Moby Dick*—then he grabs the Cliff's Notes first). You hardly ever see the Go-getter linger and lounge around unless he's planning something—and that's usually something good and fun.

The Go-getter is a forward-looking boy who is outgoing and an optimist. In short, he just goes and gets it. And "it" may include the finer points of the sports he's involved in, the purpose for being in school in the first place, or the tons of super activities teens can have fun with. There are three types of Go-getter, and they all score high on Princely potential.

The Overachiever

He's the nice, hardworking boy who's involved in almost everything and really tries in everything he does. He may not have a lot of natural talent, but he makes up for that through extra effort and by pouring all the energy he's got into whatever he does.

This boy I like never sits still. He's always coming up with stuff to sign up for, or, like, a fun way to decorate our class float. He's always at it. —Lucy Chee, 15

Sure, the Overachiever has considerable energy. You find him in the tough classes, not making the best grades, but always passing the class, even if it means retaking a quiz, asking for extra credit, or getting tutored.

You also find him on the track team or working out in the weight room, never being the top dog but *way determined* to get there. He's not the cutest guy in school either, but he sneaks a peek at GQ and teen dudes' mags and picks up on plenty of hunky hints. And he's quick about catching on, like he's another pre–American Idol Clay Aiken, who quickly learned to make the best of his so-so looks. That's the Overachiever for you—he takes what he's got and makes it a lot. And best of all, he does what he's told by parents and teachers. So he's reliable, dependable, and a good friend to his pals—be they guys or gals.

The Preppie

Here's another frequently found boy. He's way opposite from the Geek in looks and goals. While the Geek is super smart in one or two areas but maybe is still trying to figure out exactly what those areas are, the Preppie already knows what he wants out of life—often to the *n*th degree—and that is to be super prepared for a successful future! To him, that means he's got to plan for and focus on a high-paying future career. He wants to make good grades now and attend a stellar college later. And then he plans on snagging a super-good job down the road. So to get ready, the Preppie has decided to go to prep school in your school. The Preppie usually dresses like he's attending an elite prep school—in khaki shorts or creased pants, with his polo shirts tucked in, and his hair short and neat.

The Prep's usually outgoing and friendly to other kids, and also to teachers and adults. He might even know whom he'll ask for college recommendations in his freshman year of high school! So the Prep mingles well with kids your own age and with grown-ups. Frequently, the Preps are boys who seem to have skipped any awkward growth stage—no outward growing pains for them!—and have morphed into young adults early on.

The Prez

This boy has some serious general Go-getter traits mixed in with Preppie traits. That means he does a lot of things, and does a lot of them very well. In the yearbook, you'll find a super-long list of achievements under his name. And his picture is always way cute—the Prez cares about his looks, though not to the degree that the Prep does. Most of all, the Prez puts his buds first. He'll drop anything to help them out, and he'll even stretch the truth on occasion to cover for his buds. He's an organization guy, which means he's usually in a meeting at lunchtime or busy getting the word out at other times. Usually, he's an officer in more than one club. He's not always the head of the student council, but he can be. The Prez likes attention and is a real ham when he speaks in front of the class. He has tons of confidence and when he smiles, so does everyone around him. No matter what he looks like, the Prez is seen as hot. He's like a golden boy, whom everybody likes, loves, and adores.

There's this one boy I'm just crazy about. Even kids in grade school have heard of him 'cause he's so nice and cute.
—Kelsey, 13

Universal High School

Tonya had a crush on a boy who was tall, thin, and walked in sort of a lopey way. His face was the absolute *cutest*. He had perfect teeth and when he smiled, it made anyone around him smile—most of all Tonya. The boy, Benny, was Mr. Everything at her school. The coach praised him, the teachers nominated him for stuff, and all the other girls IM'ed about his every move.

Tonya noticed him the first day of school, but then she forgot about him because Benny wasn't in any of her classes. Meanwhile, she'd met some other boys, those that she ran into in Key Club meetings and during student gov sessions.

This was her junior year and she had vowed not to be shy anymore. Whenever one of the boys started talking to her, she smiled and chatted and was friendly. A few times she even went to the movies with one boy or another. But then when she saw those boys the next day, she didn't like them. In fact, she didn't want to have anything to do with them anymore. She felt uncomfortable talking to them, being around them, or holding their hands. She felt like she was just a run-of-the-mill girl to the boys.

So she only wanted one thing, to run from them and find somewhere, anywhere, to hide. She even made her best buds lie for her, just so she could keep out of those guys' eyes. "Uh, Tonya went home sick," she had her friends say, or "Tonya went home with cramps, you know." Just any excuse, so she didn't have to face any of those boys until they got the message and left her alone.

"Why do I feel this way?" Tonya asked herself. She tried to think of all kinds of explanations but everything she came up with didn't make sense. Tonya thought she'd be doomed for the rest of her life and that she'd never have a relationship with any boy. But when second semester rolled around, Benny was moved into her third-period trig class. The moment she saw him again, she felt like smacking her forehead. Benny had been in the same school all along, she just hadn't dared to really look his way 'cause he was so *popular*, but now she saw him every day.

"Slow down, girl," she told herself. "This isn't like snagging the hottest pair of shoes at Macy's." So Tonya didn't gush all over him like some of the other girls. Didn't scrape her chair closer to talk to him. Didn't hang all over his desk or follow him to his next class. No, Tonya was too smart to go overboard right away, but during class, she caught him looking at her across the room.

When she had a trig problem she couldn't do, she called one of her friends, not Benny. In class, she gave him a casual smile, stayed in her assigned seat, and waited to see what would develop.

In the meantime, she found out she got the highest grade on the midterm. After class, Benny ambled over and asked if he could see her test. He'd missed only one question but wanted to see where he'd gone wrong. And so it started, slowly and perfectly. Tonya and Benny began studying together, first only before a major exam, then before quizzes, then most every day. Instead of avoiding Benny, Tonya couldn't wait for the next time they'd put their heads together over a page of math problems.

One day, after school, a horrible storm kept everyone inside the building for an extra ten minutes so they wouldn't get drenched. A loud thunderclap scared Tonya and she practically jumped out of her skin. That's when Benny reached over and held her hand. And Tonya felt totally and absolutely comfortable with that.

Could You Be a Go-Getter Repellent?

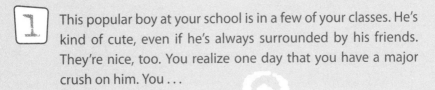

1. This popular boy at your school is in a few of your classes. He's kind of cute, even if he's always surrounded by his friends. They're nice, too. You realize one day that you have a major crush on him. You . . .

    a. Feel way thrilled. Just bumping into him in the hallways makes your whole week.

b. Practice your flirty smile in the mirror at home. When you see him in class the next day, you whisper "hi" to the back of his head.

c. Velcro yourself to him between classes and IM him tons after school.

d. Tell your best bud about your crush but say you're not going to do much about it 'cause it could pass. Your life doesn't revolve around any guys—it revolves around you!

2 This well-known boy you *really* like gave your girlfriend a piggyback ride to class the other day. She keeps bragging about it nonstop. You . . .

a. Listen to her retell the story and then daydream that it was you.

b. Pretend to hurt your ankle when he's nearby. Maybe he'll carry you or your backpack or at least point you to the nurse's office.

c. Make sure you're on opposing teams in gym class floor hockey. Then, when the time is right, you trip and fall into his arms, or at least near his feet.

d. Tell her it's a nice story, but she's told it to you already. Then you change the topic to the fun stuff on your daily planner.

3 You have been secretly admiring a super guy. You thought it was just a crush but it seems like it could be much more because now he's interested in you. You . . .

a. Keep secretly admiring him but don't let him or anyone else know about it, especially him!

b. Tell everyone in school how you feel and then spend your nights Googling his name with his picture taped to your computer screen.

c. Start planning the most romantic date ever at the coolest diner in town.

d. Tell your trusted best gal pals and ask them if they know any boys who can check out the situation.

4. One of your fab friends has suddenly discovered boys, and she has her eye on the most popular boy in your grade. She gives him love taps, hugs him, flirts constantly with him, and even chases him down the hall to tickle him! She has gone totally crazy over this boy. You . . .

a. Watch her and take notes in your diary after school. When she comes over, you leave the diary lying around and hope she'll read it so her over-the-top actions stop.

b. Feel a tad envious. You buy the hottest "How to Get a Guy" books the grownups read and think about putting the advice in them to use—someday soon.

c. Decide to play her game. So you wear your cutest crop top, keep your lips super glossed and your shiny mane ready to Rapunzel him in. You will win.

d. Nicely tell your friend she needs to chill. You let her know that overflirting could be hurting her, and if she really wants him, she needs to play it cool.

If flirting is done right and not too fast, not way in-your-face, it could eventually lead to dating. —Daley, 16

Now it's time to find out your true Crush Quotient, your CQ. Tally your answers and find the description that best fits you. If you have a mixture, look at all the breakdowns. Obviously, there's a bit of everything in you, which is fab. Now, can you work on having a little less of the answer A attitude and a little more of the answer D attitude?

Mostly A's: Shy Shania

You are excited about crushes, flirts, and potential boyfriends, but don't let that subject get you all flustered and cloistered. You're a super girl now. You don't have to scurry off any time a boy looks your way. You need to start letting people know how you feel, when you feel it.

Mostly B's: Prissy Missy

You're doing great overall. But when you're crushing on a boy, it makes you feel confused. Always know you're pretty and likable, and boys will take a look at you. You can snare anyone you want; it's no big deal.

Mostly C's: Earnest Emma

You're an aggressive girl and when you see something you want, you go for it. But jumping on any boy you like and forcing him to pay attention to you is so not going to win his affection. Use your rude warrior 'tude on the athletic field, but try to play it cooler with the boys.

If flirting isn't done correctly, it may send the wrong message. A girl can be so pushy that her crushes could think she's a pushover. That's a sure turnoff. —Mindy, 16

Mostly D's: Way Cool Jewel

You're a gem. You know that boys are out there, but they don't get to tell you what your game plan is. It's a Girls' World! You have the power to pick and choose a boy when and if you want a crush, and you feel like there's no pressure to do it.

GO-GETTER FACTORS: What Should You Know about the Go-Getter?

The wonderful news is that there are lots of Go-getters around. And they are easily recognizable by the way they look—good! and by way they act and react—friendly. So most everybody likes them.

The best thing is for a teenage girl to have a thing for a teenage boy in her school who is way acceptable. Then the stage of flirting might develop. —Tammy, 16

The Go-getter can range from a super-hardworking boy to a very ambitious boy who's a long-range planner. Watch out, he can be too goal-oriented, cash-impressed, and a touch *vain*.

Every time I run across this hunky boy that all the girls like, I notice how nice he looks. Sometimes he even looks better than me.
—Lynne, 15

Go-getters are used to getting lots of attention. From early on, they've had plenty of adults go gaga over them. So a word of warning about these princes: Go-getters can be a little self-centered, having been gushed over for eons by kindergarten teachers, club advisors, coaches, moms, dads, older sibs, and girls, girls, girls.

GO-GETTER SIZZLERS:
What You Should Do about the Go-Getter

The Go-getter is seen as a prize guy by many folks. That's because from the outside, he looks like the total package. He may be— but still, he's just a boy who's growing up. So he isn't perfect. He expects a lot from himself and from any girl he's interested in. He wants her to be similar to him.

This gung-ho guy I know wants me to, like, join in a lot of his activities too. —Carrie, 15

Go-getters do care what other guys think about them. So this isn't the kind of boy who is attracted to a wallflower girl or a girl who'd rather die than say "Hi" back to him. Go-getters expect girls to be equals in all different kinds of ways. So if this is the kind of boy you're interested in, better get busy with sports, drama, your best buddies, or with your studies.

Go-getters like to be the center of attention. Sure, they don't frown on any girls who chase them—not to the girls' faces anyway. But boys make all kinds of smart-alecky cracks about pushy girls. So it's best to go super low-key with a Go-getter and let the attachment grow.

> With the popular guys, they don't say no when some girls target them for play-fighting, blowing kisses, footsies under a table, and other mushy things they do. But in the locker room, they really trash those chicks. My brother told me. —Amanda, 15

BOY STORY—A Real-Life Story from a Girl Like You

My friend Cynthia has had a crush on Joey, who is a real nice guy and way likable, for the longest time. Quite a few girls perk up when he enters the cafeteria, but I mean Cynthia has had it super bad. She really wants to be his *friend* friend, but he has no idea that she *likes* him because she's never told him and never showed it.

We've watched her getting lovesick over this situation. So we knew we had to do *something*. I mean, who wants to see a best friend being in heart-wrenching agony every day? So we told her to make her feelings known, just say "Hi" or wave or start talking to him.

But Cynthia was like, "No, no, never. I couldn't." She turned lollipop red in the face and almost burst into tears.

So I, and the rest of the clique, took charge. First, we crank-called Joey a few times, just breathed into the phone and hung up. Then we wrote him this long, passionate letter. We put big red hearts on it, lots of lipstick kisses, some perfume, and wrote it with words like "dearest sugar-plum darling," "hunk of my heart," and "yours 4ever." We signed Cynthia's name to it and mailed it yesterday, special delivery, to his home. And now we're anxiously waiting for the happy ending!

Gina, 15

O H B O Y - M E T E R

Grade the Girls

A big fat **F** for all of you! You'll be waiting a long, long time for a happy ending. Really, what were you thinking? With friends like you, who needs enemies? Cynthia deserves so much better. To get a passing grade, and barely that, all you can do now is contact Joey and confess—fast. Tell him you're sorry about this stupid mistake; ask him to forgive you and tell him it was a way dumb prank. And then comes the harder part—to get Cynthia to forgive you. May take a long time, and who can blame her? And before you tackle that issue, make a list of what you and your friend crew should've done—so you won't make the same horrible mistake ever, ever again.

Here's a start:

1. Always remember crushes deal with feelings and feelings can be fragile. So tread very lightly and don't act like a bull in a china shop.
2. Clue Cynthia in on some subtle ways of letting her crush know that she's into him. She could say "hi" to Joey, pay more attention to him, ask his advice on some small topic in the homework, etc.
3. Let Cynthia be the one to choose which strategy she is going with. Joey's her crush, so it's her choice.
4. If she's not yet ready to make a tiny move, it's best to butt out. Friends don't force friends to do anything (unless it's for their safety).

PRINCESS PROMOTERS:
Time for Some Activity Add-Justments

Think about all the stuff you do during your day, your week, your life outside of school. Are you happy with all you do? Are you in at least one or two outside school activities or are you in so many they kind of blur together?

I'm in way too many things at school. I always feel stressed and don't even have time to catch my breath. —Sara, 14

1. If you're into too many sports, clubs, and extra classes, you may need an activity overload add-justment. Just step back and analyze your hours out of school. If you're overburdened, you may not have time to notice the funshine, so cut back.

2. If you're in too few activities, you may need to amp up your participation. Try to think of one or two new things that interest you, and work those into your day. Maybe your school has an elective that comes with an outside activity, like an art class that requires you to exhibit your collages at the annual Spring Fling. Maybe there are things you're good at already but that you could take to the next level. If you're afraid you can't do something better, you won't ever know unless you try.

The best way to meet lots of Go-getters is to be out there where they are—running track or working out to make a varsity squad. —Carol, 15

Good advice, Carol, but don't go into something *just because of the boys.* One girl signed up to become a football trainer just so she could be closer to the hot guys. She hated her trainer chores, found getting the Gatorade a bore, and didn't last long.

Of course, if you're really interested in sports medicine down the road, or even if you just love being around the team and traveling with them, then that's something else.

3. The more you get involved in your community, the more boys you will meet, and since the Go-getters are such a large majority, the odds of your coming into contact with them go way up. So get out there and DO something!

Boy Secrets

While the Go-getters aren't shy, they prefer to meet girls who don't fall all over boys as soon as they meet them.

> I like for girls to play it cool, or try to anyway. I don't want the girl I like to hop right up and sprint on over and plunk down right next to me. Maybe later, but not first thing. —Rob, 16

Go-getters are usually pretty popular in school. So they're used to attention from a lot of people. If you act uninterested in a Go-getter, his interest might shoot through the roof because he sees it as a challenge to get a super girl like you to like him.

> When I see a girl I like passing by and she's busy with her friends and so not concerned with me, I automatically smile. To me, this is someone I might be drawn to, someone I maybe can daydream about all day long and never get tired of. —Sam, 16

Getting the attention of a Go-getter can mean downplaying or even hiding your attraction to him. In that way, crushing on a Go-getter is the opposite of shopping. When you shop, you see something you like, and if the $ is right, you snap it up. With a Go-getter, you want to window-shop. You see something you like, and look at it occasionally, but you don't do anything about it.

Keep in mind that Go-getters are surrounded by plenty of girls who admire them openly. Seems unfair that you have to hide what's inside, but it could be the way to really see if your Go-getter crush likes you back.

> My secret about what girl I crush on? She's not the one texting me 24/7. She's one giving me <u>that look</u> along with a shy smile. —Kurt, 17

That look is just looking a little longer than usual, but not staring or glaring or gaping.

So when you want a Go-getter, you don't need to be rude or totally off-putting. Hints work. You just don't need to broadside him with your affection—and this actually goes for a lot of guy types out there.

I like a little hint that the girl likes me. Then I start playing games. Like when I have a class with this girl and the teacher tells us to share our reading textbook with someone. If it just so happens that it's <u>her</u>, I'll "accidentally" drop the book on the floor. Then both of us attempt to pick it up and I manage to brush against her hand. —Frankie, 15

Boy File

Get out your file cards and head up a dozen of them "Go-getters." Using the Crush Code, write down the code names (as explained on page 31) of the popular boys at your school. Then, put them into subcategories. Which ones are the Overachievers? Which ones are the Preppies? Which ones are the Prez types and Prez wannabes? Write down what makes them that. What makes them so special to most people? List their activities, achievements, projects, prospects, sports—all their great goings-on. On the back of the card, write down what you find so attractive about them.

And then on another card or in your diary, write down what is so attractive *about you*. Just write down all your superlative qualities, whether they're out in the open or not. If you can't think of a lot of great ways to describe yourself, think harder!

Do any of the Go-getters in your school have girlfriends you like and respect? If they do, study these girls from now on to see what traits they have that might make them a good match for the Go-getters. Write these traits down. There may be a few of those traits that wouldn't hurt for you to kinda learn from, you know? Maybe one of the girlfriends is a really good team player, even if she's not the best athlete. Can't hurt to be more of a team player!

Final Exam

So how does the Go-getter stack up? Take a look at page 33 in Chapter 3 for the report card breakdown info.

The Go-getter's Report Card

Looks: P, always
Schoolwork: P, though not every subject
Attitude: P
Behavior: F, can be a little too vain or be overly influenced by outward appearances
Activities: P, always!

Added up, that means the Go-getter gets only 1 F. That puts his Prince-for-you potential at powerful. The Go-getter is definitely a Prince in the making.

So check out the Go-getters in your life. They've got potential, and as of now, they can certainly act like Princes.

CHAPTER 5

The Prince, aka the Real Deal

The Princes in your world are just like you—'tweens or teens—except that you're a girl, and they come in a male version. That means Princes are special boys, just like you are a special girl. And they're not hard to spot. Fact is, most Princes are just a little more mature than their classmates. Other Princes are typical boys, but they all have a good belief system, good manners (or are working on 'em), are smart and capable, and yet are *not conceited at all!*

A Prince is really a great mixture of the Geek and the Go-getter. He has some talents or is trying to develop some. He likes people and is open to meeting more. He has friends, at least one or two or three, and he's pretty secure with himself. He's unselfish and not constantly trying to impress.

A lot of times, the Prince has already overcome some personal challenges, so he doesn't come across as spoiled, bratty, self-centered, or superficial. Some Princes have it rough. They have jobs after school, or come from single-parent homes and have to look after younger sibs. Or sometimes their dads and moms work two jobs, so the Princes have to step up at home.

Many Princes are just more grownup than other boys their age, and wow—that's what's so nice about them, because *you're* more grownup than a lot of other girls and boys your age. Princes seem so *real*, because they are, and best of all, they like girls. They like you!

What Makes a Boy a Prince?

LeShaun is a member of the baseball team and the History Club, and he's a homeroom rep—but clubs aren't his whole life. He attends the meetings unless something else comes up, but most often it's only to promote and help his friends become the frontrunners in any activity. LeShaun doesn't want or need the hassles or honors of being best in anything—not that he couldn't be, if he tried.

LeShaun knows that he doesn't have to prove himself over and over. He's quite secure where he's at and doesn't have to go for any medals. He's pretty settled in his life and cool in so many ways. He's not perfect but he may be a perfect *friend* friend for you. You see, he is at the right stage of his life—the right stage for you. That means, he is growing and going places, just like you. At the same time, he's fab and fun to be around and there's a lot of give and take between him and you—in school, after the last bell when it's time for that sometimes sooo boring student council meet, or at the lake, where the 4-H picnic's going to be.

One example: Just yesterday, during that snooze-city assembly for the whole school when you thought you'd just about drop off into a day-long slumber that would freak out your homeroom teach, who gets such a kick out of "her" students being the way best-behaving kids around, LeShaun sent you a wake-up call, sorta. What he did, even sitting three rows behind you, was pass an elbow nudge along with the instructions that it be forwarded on to you with the message, "LeShaun says, don't yawn."

So of course, you immediately perked up and sat up super straight.

It made your teacher's day. Hey, even more key, it made yours. LeShaun literally had your back.

One thing for sure, he is a Prince.

Dear Dr. Erika:

I feel a connection with this boy on my track team. Secretly, I've liked for him for a long time. What I like about him besides his looks is that he doesn't give up. Like last year when he sprained his ankle and couldn't do the long jump, he came to practice anyway. He hobbled onto the practice field and was never late. He didn't expect any special treatment; he just showed up and helped out the other guys with advice and stuff. Even spent time telling me how I can cut, like, whole seconds off my hurdling time. And he was and is way patient and, like, always praises me. Wow!

Chloe, 14

Dear Dr. Erika:

I've had a boyfriend for two years, which is a really, *really* long time in high school. Anyway, four weeks ago I kissed another guy. This guy was just a friend. It happened at a party, and it didn't mean anything. Anyway, to make a long story short, I told my boyfriend because I couldn't live with the guilt. I begged him to forgive me and finally he did but told me not to ever go back to the other guy's house again. I agreed.

Then three weeks ago, my boyfriend kissed another girl. He told me about it, saying it just happened, didn't mean anything, and I forgave him and didn't break up with him.

I didn't tell him to stop talking to this girl altogether because I thought I could trust him not to do anything else. That made him realize that forbidding me to go to the other guy's house ever again was a sign of his not trusting me. So he said I could go over there if I wanted to. And from then on, we decided to talk more openly and that got our good relationship back on track. Before then, we'd been talking about getting engaged in college and getting married after we went to grad school.

Now we realized that was way *silly*. Why live in a dream world when the *now* is so great? So filled with all kinds of opportunities! We're just going to see what happens with us in the future. Meanwhile, we'll continue to be boyfriend-girlfriend but not heavy-like, and we'll work out whatever issues come up. We'll take it as it comes, and talk about what bothers us.

                                                    Tanishea, 16

Sounds as if both girls are dealing with a Prince! And you know what? The special pay-off of that is, involving yourself with a Prince, even just as a friend, makes you develop more super traits. Prince behavior rubs off; it transfers, like a lingering aroma. Have you ever stored a sweater in a cedar chest? Well, if you have, you know it comes out smelling nice and heavenly, not moth-bally at all. Same here. Hanging with a Prince is priceless, 'cause no matter what, you plain end up being nicer yourself. It's like osmosis—you know, that old word from science class that means the tendency to "absorb something from another." In this case, it's something positive.

F Y I

The Princes are a big group of boys in your school. They come in all kinds of wrappings, from boy-next-door looks and likable, to super cute and smart to boot.

This way nice guy at school never pushes himself on anyone. He's cool, just there to be a friend or to have a little crush on.
— Jennifer, 14

Yes, the Princes aren't out there selling themselves constantly like the Go-getters like to do.

This one boy I like really listens to me when I tell him something and next day he remembers and he's, like, "Did you, like, solve it—whatever your prob was?" —Zackie, 15

Also, Princes don't have their heads in the clouds like a lot of the Geeks do. They aren't absentminded or preoccupied with their latest computer game scores.

Princes make good grades and are school-involved to a certain degree, but they don't go overboard. They don't have to. They already have a lot of things figured out, and one of those things is that they like their lives and themselves just fine, most days anyway.

Princes feel no need to hurry through their teens and be pseudo–Wall Street brokers or Junior Chairmen of the Board now. The Princes are comfortable and they make girls comfortable too.

A Prince has strong character. He won't go cause trouble with other boys. And he would never, ever drag a girl into his problems if he did make a mistake.

These nice boys at my school hardly ever get in trouble. If they do, it's no biggie, just, like, toilet-papering a car with their buddies. —Madeline, 15

Yes, Princes are, most of all, nice boys. They aren't 100 percent perfect, but they do the right things and they back up their buds, be they boys or girls. A Prince believes in himself and in you. Being around him is always way reassuring. You know he's on your side. He's like your best girl pal, but male.

Around a Prince you feel safe and protected. Sure, he may try a little something now and then if he's crushing on you, but he'll never do anything you don't want to or aren't ready for. He respects you and is willing to go along with your plans. A Prince understands that teen life can be tricky and that growing up can be confusing, but he refuses to be bummed out about everything.

Princes see the future as bright, they give you hope when you're down, and they compliment and complement you.

Universal High School

After a year of crushing on older guys and getting a taste of their mannerisms toward younger girls, Alley decided she was way above that and too smart for them. At the end of ninth grade, a year of complete transition, she started talking to a guy named Dane, a boy in her grade. He was so different from all of the other boys—sweet, not pushy, and just so much fun. She thought he was quite a catch, and they ended up spending a lot of time together.

They had a lot of the same classes, so they could help each other out with homework and stuff. In second period when Alley struggled with a difficult exercise in Spanish II, she could relax, knowing that after school, Dane would help her with the toughest passage. It was super to have a top study buddy, but he was more than that. Dane was Alley's *friend* friend. And so it went, both of them even sat next to each other whenever possible, except for sixth period, when they were in different classes.

Even more enjoyable was after school and being on the cross-country team together. Dane always finished first with his warm-ups, but Alley was no slouch either. She was the leader of the girls' squad. Since there was only one coach for this sport, the girls and guys ran together.

All that changed when Kadi enrolled. Kadi was a new girl, tall and older, and with the most gorgeous clothes Alley had ever seen. Nothing but high-fashion jeans and soft, clingy cashmere tops, wool miniskirts and shearling vests. And she drove a chocolate-brown Mercedes Benz convertible, with the top down even when it got chilly. Everyone in school talked about nothing but Kadi for weeks, and the worst thing was, she was put into Dane's sixth-period class.

Alley didn't *really* care. Oh, sure, she did about the clothes and stuff; she wished she had money to get her gear from someplace else besides Target once in a while, but that wasn't it. She started hearing about how Kadi was snagging every guy in school. The most popular couples that had been going together for months suddenly broke up because of Kadi, according to rumor, not that Alley actually saw it firsthand. Still, all that gossiping made her a little nervous—but just a little.

One day, the topic of trust just came up between Dane and Alley. Dane said that she could always trust him. And Alley said that he could always trust her. It was like a promise of sorts, the way both of them said it. Loud and clear, looking into each other's eyes, and not laughing or anything.

One day, Dane walked Alley to Gina's car. Gina lived next door to Alley and took her to and from school every day. Dane and Alley were talking, and when it was time to go, Dane accidentally left his backpack next to Gina's car. So Alley tossed it into Gina's trunk, and then called Dane on his cell phone to let him know where the backpack was. Then it was forgotten.

The next morning, Alley was putting her backpack into Gina's trunk when she noticed Dane's and brought it up to the front seat with her. Gina and Alley left for school, and as they were driving along, Alley glanced at the bag and Gina glanced at Alley. This game went on for some time. Finally, Alley couldn't stand it anymore; she wanted to go though the bag so bad! Gina knew that was what Alley had been thinking the entire ride. So they both started laughing, pulled over, and dug in like crazy. At first they found just the usual contents, and Alley felt ridiculous for her childish curiosity. Then, as she rummaged through the pens, pencils, and scrap paper in the front pocket, she found a letter in a small, worn leather wallet. "Aha!" she shouted with a laugh, thinking the letter was from her. She opened it and this is what it said:

Hey Hottie,

Of all the guys I met since I got here, you're the only

one that rocks my world. And you know it. But lately

you seem to avoid me. When I called you last night, you

couldn't get off the phone fast enough. When I I.M'ed you,

you blocked me. When I texted you, nothing. So OK, I'm

giving you <u>one more chance</u>. Meet me in front of the gym

at 8 A.M. Tues.! Kadi

After reading every word—twice—Gina started the motor again and the girls drove to school without saying a word. It was almost 8:00 A.M. They ran breathless to the gym, with Alley in front, feeling terrible about having snooped and about spying on Dane. . . . And just so incredibly furious that he would have done that—how could he?

They saw Kadi with her clique and a bunch of hip guys, a kid named Roy in the middle and cracking a joke, but no Dane.

The bell rang and the girls had to go to class, but Alley was poised to let Dane have it. Not a second longer was she going to wait to make him fess up. When he slipped into his seat next to hers, she hissed, "Man, we gotta talk."

"All right," he said, his eyebrows rising at her irate tone of voice. "But first, where's my backpack?"

Alley wanted to tell him how she had flung the thing out of the window of the car as they drove, but before she could get the words out, Dane said, "Got to give Roy back his wallet. He left it in the bathroom yesterday and I picked it up. Now what do you want to talk about?"

Alley swallowed, trying to think of a way out. "It's about your bag," she said eventually, in a completely different tone of voice. "It kinda sorta fell out of the car. . . ."

Then she caught herself. *No. No lies,* she thought. *Trust is a must,* she thought. *I just have to come clean and hope that Dane can forgive me. Certainly, making up a big fat tale to cover up what I did is only going to make things worse.*

"Actually . . . ," she started hesitantly, and then she began to tell him exactly what had happened. All the while she watched his face, expecting to see a big frown appear, or a wave of irritation flash across it, or his eyes to show he was angry. She figured he would turn away from her in disappointment or disgust.

Instead, he listened, and then he grabbed her hand, squeezed it, and laughed out loud. "You don't know how many times," he said, "I've been tempted to go through your purse. Almost did once. I opened it but just then you came back in the room. So no big deal, we're both guilty, and we've both got a lot of talking and apologizing to do. Me first, of course, I did wrong first. But now, where exactly did you pitch my backpack out the window?"

Sometimes you have to have a little bad in a <u>friend</u> friendship to go along with the good, to even things out. And test it. Surviving the bad, the tough stuff, makes your relationship with a good guy stronger. —Sunni, 16

Could You Be a Prince Repellent?

 There's just something about this boy you like in your drama class. Thinking about him makes you smile, and your heart beats faster because of the way he walks and talks. He seems a little shy, though. You . . .

    a. Use your newfound acting skills to hide your giddy feelings. You go around looking tragic, humming a sad song, and hoping this will inspire him to get up the nerve to ask you what's wrong.

    b. Think, "Wow!" You're so thrilled to have him in your life. You clue in your clique and send them spying on him. Throughout the day, they text or pass notes to you about what he's doing.

c. Ask him if he wants to practice a kissing scene from *Romeo and Juliet* at your house, over and over and over . . .

d. Realize that you're having an epic crush and enjoy the sensation. If the right opportunity presents itself, you'll say "hi" to him, but it's not your #1 priority.

2 You find yourself daydreaming about the really cool boy in your homeroom. Your friends want to tell the guy's buddies about how you feel. You . . .

a. Get really annoyed at them for even considering this and wish you hadn't told them. But since they will probably be offended if you say no, you just choose not to even talk about it anymore.

b. Wait till he leaves the room to go to the bathroom, then have your friends tape a note with your name and number to the back of his notebook.

c. Shout, "Finally! It's about time." You instruct your friends to print up a hot resumé of yourself, including your best pic and deliver it to him.

d. Tell your friends to mention it casually, in passing, if the topic comes up. Meanwhile, you keep moving ahead with your schedule and your busy life.

3 This friendly guy in sixth period always glances at you from across the room but never says anything. He seems to have a lot of friends he is always gabbing with, even when he is sneaking peeks at you. You . . .

a. Move your seat—as far away as possible. You don't like boys staring at you, no matter how nice they are! Why can't you be invisible?

b. Glance at him casually, as you let your eyes roam around the room. All the other boys get a split-second look, but he gets a longer, passionate one. Can you say *smolder*?

c. Open up your arsenal and use your best weapons—you bat your eyes, lick your lips, giggle and jiggle, and move your desk closer every day. No way will he even *look* at other girls in the class.

d. Look at him once in a while too, and smile. The rest is up to him. If he likes you, he can make the next move. If he doesn't, that's okay too.

 4 Your boyfriend is taking Driver's Ed, a class that shows a lot of movies. There's a girl in there with a huge crush on him even though she knows he's got a girlfriend—you. She always messes with his hair, brushes against him, and flirts with him. You . . .

a. Act like you know nothing about what's going on. Only when you pull the bed covers over your head at night do you let yourself cry about it.

b. Ask your boyfriend if he'll move his seat away from her or to the front so the teacher can see this jerky girl's behavior and make her stop.

c. Are. So. Annoyed. You're mad at your boyfriend, mad at that hussy, mad at the teacher! When you see that girl in school, you're so going to . . . !

d. Ask your boyfriend about the girl who's lusting after him and see what he says. You can tell if he's innocent about it. Ask him what he's going to do to get her to stop. You're trustworthy, so you expect him to be too.

> Now it's time to find out your true Crush Quotient, your CQ. Tally your answers and find the description that best fits you. If you have a mixture, look at all the breakdowns. Obviously, there's a bit of everything in you, which is fab. Now, can you work on having a little less of the answer A attitude and a little more of the answer D attitude?

Mostly A's: Mini Melissa

Stop always minimizing yourself and take your rightful place in your world. You are a great girl and don't need to constantly hide or fade away or close your eyes. Stand tall and let others know that you're not afraid. You can handle anyone.

Mostly B's: Flip-flop Flora

You're getting there, but make sure you don't backtrack. When you have a *friend* friend, you almost always deal with various situations in a straight-forward manner, which is definitely on track! Be careful you don't go over-board in your bluntness. It's OK to tell it like it is, as long as you are not hurting others' feelings.

Mostly C's: Desperate Delia

Halloween is once a year, so why do you act demonic all the time? No need to constantly freak out over a boy or over life in general. You are bright and smart, so don't sabotage yourself all the time by overreacting.

Mostly D's: Cool Christina

Congratulations to you for keeping calm in the eye of the boy storm. You know that it's nice to have boys like you, but you aren't letting them take over your whole life. Too much to do and too much fun ahead, so if a *friend* friendship happens, great. If not, there are other fish in the sea!

PRINCE FACTORS:
What Should You Know about the Prince?

Look around you—there are Princes all over the place! They vary in cuteness, just like nice girls do. They shine in some subjects and just hang in there in others. They play a sport or two, and overall just try to make it through the day the best way they can.

> This one nice boy I know has trouble with Intro Chemistry too. That makes me like him even better 'cause I feel we're on the same level. —Sherma, 15

Princes can have their bad days, even an off week sometimes. A Prince may not turn in every essay on time or he may be late to class occasionally, but the true good qualities of the Prince will always shine through.

The diff between a super guy and a so-so one is: The super guy makes a mistake, but only once—and he apologizes. Not like some dunce who keeps on making the same mistake over and over.
—Cristina, 15

If you want to meet a Prince, be a Princess! Princes like girls who are good matches.

My bro, who's a super-great guy, likes girls that are like the type of guy who won't hog the ball in soccer. —Lois, 13

That means Princes like girls who are nice, friendly, and good sports. Princes go for girls who are real and who tell the truth and try to always do the right thing.

PRINCE SIZZLERS:
What You Should Do about the Prince

Since the Prince has few problems besides the usual ones, and he isn't in serious trouble, you want to make sure you are dealing with whatever comes up in your life, too, and not sweep it under the rug. See your guidance counselor if you feel like you have a huge problem and you don't know how to deal with it.

Princes like being teenagers, so don't try to act past your age, like some mature siren. You're not that way and you don't have to be that way, so be yourself! You'll be a grown-up for most of your life, so enjoy the age you're at. Don't change yourself to impress a Prince. He hates phonies, hates being fussed over, and hates for a girl to fake liking something he likes.

It's way relaxing to be around this great guy I know. There's just something that lights up in me when he's around. I feel safe and don't have to, like, pretend with him. —Martina, 16

The Prince likes girls who are doers—not just total wishers, if-only-ers, and procrastinators. Princes are participants in the world unfurling around them and they like girls who are the same. So just do the best you can do and watch him take notice of you. The best part is, you'll feel better about yourself even if he doesn't notice! If you always act like a baby and you throw a lot of hissy fits, the Prince (and other people, too) may end up thinking you're either plain rude or just too immature for him.

BOY STORY—A Real-Life Story from a Girl Like You

When I was fourteen, I had a serious crush on a boy. His name was Ryan and he was a sophomore. We met at a wrestling match in the high school gym. He was a wrestler and I was the assistant team manager. I had just transferred to this high school, so I welcomed every friendly smile sent my way. Ryan was sweet and kind, like a big brother, really. He showed me the school, walked me to my classes, talked with me during breaks at wrestling tournaments, and became my best friend.

As our friendship became even stronger my crush became a mega one. Ryan was so wonderful and treated me so well that I began thinking about him, like, almost 24/7. When I did my homework, before I could even write the first word of my book report on *Brave New World* or anything, I found my hand going crazy and making all these intertwined hearts and, like, writing Ryan's name about a gazillion times. Sure, I had had a crush once before, but the intensity of my feelings this time made my previous crush seem so lame!

Actually I was afraid to even let Ryan know how I felt, 'cause I figured he just viewed me as a good friend, kinda like his baby sister and nothing more. I was totally afraid he didn't feel the same way, so I kept my mouth shut. How happy was I when Ryan finally told me he was majorly crushing on me too! From then on, we talked on the phone and IM'ed every day and found out that we had even more things in common. Both of us started pushing ourselves a little more 'cause we wanted to be better, and not just to impress the other person but to kind of stretch our wings and see what we could accomplish if we tried.

See, the whole world was ours 'cause we weren't star-crossed, like Romeo and Juliet. We were star-*crushed*. That means, we were meant to be really good friends who are way compatible and super comfy with each other, and we didn't leave out other friends in the process, either. Everyone, even Ryan's dog, Parker, was really happy Ryan and I liked each other so much and got along so well.

Then, one day Ryan got this letter in the mail. It was from the School of Math and Science in Durham, North Carolina, a place for kids to finish their last two years of high school. It's kind of like going to college early. Durham, North Carolina, was far away from where we lived, and Ryan would have to go to boarding school there. So that was the worst news—and the best, in a way. Graduates from that school really have, like, the whole world in front of them.

All Ryan was worried about was how I'd take it. I cried, sure, but not for too long. This was *it* for Ryan, a great step toward the super future he had in mind. I knew that being star-crushed means being up there with the stars and being so happy and stuff, and this was something Ryan had always wanted.

So I got over my tears and threw him an awesome going-away party. I invited all of our friends and the whole wrestling team and the coaches and teachers Ryan had had since kindergarten. We had a blast, and whenever I felt myself getting teary-eyed, I just grabbed a bunch of tissues. And you know what? The week after Ryan left, I got a letter too. This one was from the School of the Arts in Winston-Salem, North Carolina. They said for me to submit some of my artwork for consideration for acceptance in the future! This school is for kids who like art as much as Ryan likes science.

So, man, did I have lots to e-mail, IM, and call Ryan about. And he always got back to me right away. Now our crush was long distance but cruisin'.

Six months later (just about a week ago!), I got another letter—*accepted*! It means that I'll finish my junior and senior years in a place even farther away from my Ryan, but that's OK. Whenever I look at the night sky, I just pick out two twinkly stars that are close and wish on them.

Who knows what the future has in store? Meantime, I got lots to work on and lots to learn.

Whitney, 15

OH BOY-METER

Grade the Girls

A big A+++ to you, Whitney, for being so loving and having so much common sense. Sure, you could've pitched a hissy fit when Ryan went off to that residential high school. Or you could've gotten down in the dumps and felt sooo sorry for yourself. But no, you didn't stand in Ryan's way; you rejoiced in his success, and see what happened? Success came your way too, girl. Wow!

When you meet a Prince guy, your confidence soars, because he makes you more independent, more sure of yourself and strong.
—Jenn, 15

Yes, every time you meet a Prince, you feel more empowered. A Prince makes you more courageous, more daring, more ready to take on the whole world.

PRINCESS PROMOTERS: Time for Some Accessory Add-Justments

These add-justments are fun and simple. All you have to do is focus on your accessories and put in place a few minor accessory add-justments. You're already a Princess, doing all the right things, so this is just an added bonus!

1. First of all, toss out or donate to Goodwill (or your younger sister or cousin!) any accessories that you've outgrown, that are out of style, or that are broken. You know, the lame scarves, the shabby-but-not-chic-anymore purse, and the cracked headband. Add a sequined band, floral barrettes, and feathery or suede hair ties. This'll make doing your hair much more fun, even when you're on the run!

2. Accessorize your space. Buy yourself a little plant or pick some fresh flowers to add some positive power to your room or any room in the house.

3. Once a week, add something to the family dinner, without being nagged to do it. Set the table extra-nice, put some flowers in the middle of it, or even make something to eat! Being a Princess doesn't just mean you improve yourself little by little, but that you do a little something special for the rest of the gang too.

Boy Secrets

How does a Prince react to a girl who has made an impression on him?

> When I see a nice girl that I'm interested in, I just start talking to her. First I give her a look to put her on notice that I'm crushing and then I see what happens next. —Jeremy, 16

Usually, what happens after that look either attracts a Prince further or turns him off. If the girl accepts the look for what it is—just a look, nothing else—and carries on with whatever she's doing, the Prince may continue to be interested in her. But if a girl starts to get all fluttery, flirty, and overbearing, it can totally backfire on her.

My top secret is—if a girl acts like she's Paris Hilton, I'm so not going to make the effort to get to know her. I really don't like girls that act over-the-top. —Lane, 16

Princes are just not into really obvious, and occasionally obnoxious, flirting. They would rather get to know a girl as a friend first. And then later, if there is a spark, the Prince can become a boyfriend!

Flirting, in my opinion, is when you test someone to see if she's interested in you and if you're into her. Flirting is different for everyone. It also depends on the situation you're in. If both people are the athletic type, then the guy might play ball against her so he'll win, but right at the end he lets the girl win, or vice versa. —Jon, 15

The Prince likes to drop subtle hints. He rarely chases you down like you're a bus pulling away from the stop and he's running desperately late. But when you need him or have something on your mind, the Prince is a friend who's there to hear you out.

I start out with just casually talking to a girl I'm attracted to. But this doesn't have to be just talking to be talking. It can be offering to help carry her science project or band instrument or tennis stuff. Or just picking up her book bag and lugging it to wherever she's going. —Bert, 15

Boy File

Get out your trusty stack of note cards and head up a bunch of them "Princes." List the names of any boys you know who fall into this category. These boys don't have to be the hottest or the smartest or the best athletes. They just have to be boys who you feel comfortable around.

If you can't think of too many Princes right off, it just means you'll have fun ahead! Sit back and let your mind wander. Imagine a shop where all kinds of boy qualities are put out on shelves: personalities, hair color, eye color, height, smarts, and hearts. What kind of boy would be your Prince if you could put him together out of various parts from the Ultimate Prince Store? Make the boy of your dreams! (You may need to switch to your diary for this one.) Maybe you can describe half a dozen dream guys not only from the outside, but also what they'd be like inside.

Get your fab friends and best buds together and have them write down what Princely qualities they'd love to see in potential *friend* friends. Just remember, you and your buds should never gab about this around the boys themselves!

It's really important to figure out the inner qualities you want in your eventual *friend* friend. Special gift wrapping is great, but it's what's inside the gift box that rocks the most! Underneath the Prince's looks, there has to be a Prince heart.

Final Exam

Overall, once you learn how to spot a Prince, you've got it made for the rest of your life. Why? Well, let's just grade the Prince, then you'll see for yourself. (Take a look at page 33 in Chapter 3 for the report card breakdown info.)

The Prince's Report Card

Looks: P
Schoolwork: P
Attitude: P
Behavior: P
Activities: P

Added up, that means the Prince gets 0 **F**'s. That puts his Prince-for-you potential in the perfect-for-you category. Yay!

Check out the Princes in your life. They're super guys and there's usually a lot of them around. Once you can spot them, you can relax and forget the rest of the guys. The Prince knows you're a great girl, not a Barbie Doll or Wonder Woman or Girl Genius. You are just you, *wonderful you*!

> So if he's really a Prince, he'll let you explain if you do something wrong, and together you can work out your problems. You'll listen to him, he'll listen to you—that's what Princes do. Thank you for sharing all these secrets on worthwhile boys. Saved me years of aggravation! Now I'm boy smart and I know which boys are keepers. —September, 16

PART III

The Bogus Boys: The Frogs

ow for the bad news: Maybe 25 percent of the boys you meet will *not* be bonus boys like you read about in Part II. So to weed out the definite bad-news boys, who may range from minor annoyances to real weirdos, you have to know all about them and their habits and habitats.

It takes only one bad experience with a no-good guy to mar and scar you. But if you know what to look out for, you can steer clear of these bad apples and not let them spoil the whole harvest!

> I met this way cool dude in ninth grade who had me fooled, like, totally. He ruined my sophomore and junior years and I'm still hurting bad. I'll never make this mistake again. —Marquita, 17

Fortunately, you have only three types of bogus boys to steer clear of—read on to learn who they are!

CHAPTER 6

The Flunky

The first type of bogus boy is the Flunky. This is the most frequent type of boy you're better off avoiding. The best way to describe this type of boy is by calling him sooo *annoying*. That's 'cause he always gets on your nerves, and with such regularity it's amazing. Oh, and he gets on everyone else's nerves too!

BOY WATCH: What Makes a Boy a Flunky?

You can always tell when Gord shows up at school, even though he sneaks in through the side door in the cafeteria or sidles down the hall. That's 'cause he's actually looking for attention. Someone always spots him and then the ripples of laughter start from one bunch of boys to the next. They all make fun of Gord. He's wearing what the rest of the guys wear, large T-shirt and blue jeans and sneaks, but he never gets the combo right. His shirt is way too big and has a dumb logo on it, while his jeans are brand-new but too short and too tight.

His hair stands straight up as if he's stuck his finger in a socket. He always loses his glasses, so he squints constantly. Breakfast, lunch, snacks—everything ends up smeared on his chin or his clothes. But Gord's prob, the reason why everyone laughs at him, is his goofy, lonely, needy expression.

So maybe your first instinct is to feel sorry for Gord. But then you realize that he isn't *really* a sad boy or an outcast nobody likes. He's a boy who loves his position as class Flunky. He works at it. He actually *enjoys* being so annoying! Proof? Any attempts anyone makes to help him get with it are completely ignored. In fact, any friendly gesture shown to him is ignored. The Flunky, who may not be blessed with good looks, could look much better if he'd only try.

It's like he *tries* to be clumsy and trip over your desk. His cheek's always dotted with toilet-paper bits where he cut himself shaving, even though he doesn't have a beard yet. But worse is the way he sounds—all stammery. Sure, lots of teenage boys can be awkward, but the Flunky has a trademark on Klutz. He gets right in your face when he talks. He has a runny nose but doesn't use a tissue, he drops everything, and he even forgets what day of the week it is—and these are his best qualities.

Gord really does look like he wants to be taken care of, supported, and babied. But he only seems like a prime candidate for a makeover. Yes, the Flunky can have a touch of cuteness about him, but he's a sure *loser*. He's a social misfit, a fumbler and bumbler—on purpose! Nothing ever goes right for him, and he whines about it rather than changing it. If you got graded in lunch, the Flunky would even fail that!

Dear Dr. Erika:
This way weird guy at school keeps following me around and staring at me, like I'm a Rodin statue in a museum. He never says anything, just gapes with his mouth open, and everyone laughs at him. Worse, they laugh at me because of it. So I told one of my friends to tell his friends to get him to stop doing that. Guess what, now he's even worse. He won't leave me alone!

Jaynie, 14

Dear Dr. Erika:

When our science teacher puts us in groups to work on a special project, I shiver 'cause she always puts this one dorky guy in with my friends and me. This is a guy nobody likes, because he acts like a freak. . . . No, that's harsh—he acts like he *wants* to get on your last nerve, though. If you tell him to stop making a noise, he'll just do it over and over.

But we never complained when he was in the group with us. We took him in, talked to him, even gave him the easiest part of the work to do. All he had to do was type the final report. Guess what? On the day of our presentation, he pulled out the notes I'd given him, all grimy and with ketchup stains on them, and started reading them aloud, mispronouncing every word. Just being a total goof-off, and not even try-ing to do a passable job. It's like he's always trying out for "American Nerd."

Alisa, 15

Sounds as if both girls are dealing with the Flunky. But you can deal with this prob. You can get the Flunky and his co-Flunky buds off your back. Just read on—this chapter has all the answers you need to help you nix any annoying Flunky behaviors, fast.

FYI

In some ways, the Flunky is like the Geek, but in none of the good ways. The Geek can be out to lunch, but he'll get a clue when you tell him what's what. The Flunky does the opposite—the more you try to help him out, the worse he gets. And where the Geek always has at least one subject or one special talent in which he excels, the Flunky has none.

You and your friends, and even the teachers, try talking to the Flunky and get nowhere. The Flunky uses all his energy to attract attention the wrong way. He grins when you tell him what he did wrong. He can also be a Gross Guy, who never evolved after age four. When most boys make a gross noise now and then, they say, "Excuse me." With a Flunky, *excuse me* is like a phrase from a foreign language. And *sorry* is not in his vocab either!

Universal High School

The week before Valentine's Day, Ayden enrolled at Universal High School. Everything was new and kind of scary for Ayden, but she immediately met three girls she liked a lot, and the classes were okay. She was ahead in some, and behind in others, but overall she fit right in.

To Ayden, Valentine's Day at her new school seemed to be a brag-fest. Everyone was holding their breath and watching what the girls got on February 14. A single red carnation or one balloon meant a girl was all right. Roses and a few balloons meant she was more popular and *really* all right. Huge bouquets, teddy bears, and Candygrams meant she was the most loved, most admired chick that everybody talked about for the rest of the year. Not getting anything was the worst; it meant nobody liked you and you were a *total zero,* and the pressure was *intense.*

This custom had gotten so out of hand recently that many girls just skipped that day and stayed home. Some of the girls sent themselves flowers or had their parents try to help. But nasty rumors started flying if the gift senders weren't actual students. Not getting anything was way awful, but for the whole school to find out that something had been sent by parents or even the girl herself, *that* made the girl a total outcast.

V-Day arrived and it was even *bigger* than Ayden's new friends had described it. Truck after truck unloaded in front of the school, and by lunchtime, epic bouquets of vibrant flowers, boxes of chocolates, balloons, banners, and beribboned teddy bears crowded the auditorium stage. All this loot would be delivered to the girls *during class.*

Fortunately, Ayden was out of it. As the new chick on the block, nobody expected her to get an armload of anything. She admired what her new friends received and sighed with relief that she was in the clear. Her sighs turned to groans when she found out part two of the Valentine's tradition was a dance and anyone who was anyone had to go. She couldn't get out of this one. Yikes! Where was she going to come up with a date on such short notice? She hadn't even fully settled into her new school yet.

There was one boy in homeroom who had kind of latched on to her. He was awkward and goofy and usually had ink all over his T-shirt. Seemed like he wore the same tee every day and the other kids didn't really like him much. That might have been because Steve was a twelfth grader still in a ninth-grade homeroom. But Ayden didn't notice all this stuff yet 'cause she was new! She didn't know that in three years he hadn't gotten enough credits to at least be a sophomore.

Ayden just saw Steve as a clownish guy who was falling all over himself in his daily mad dash to sit next to her. He kept knocking her books off her desk and stumbled over the trashcan when he came late into the room—which was every day. And when the teacher shook her head and said, "This is your *last* warning for being tardy," he'd say, "What? Who, me? What're you talking about? Why is everybody always giving me a hard time?" Not actually rude, but it was funny how out of it he was.

When Steve mumbled something about her going with him, Ayden actually felt sorry for him. She felt really pressured from her new crew, and all anyone was talking about was the dance, so why not? she figured. They tried to warn her that he was a wince instead of a Prince, but Ayden, being a tad hard-headed, decided to give him the benefit of the doubt.

After school, Steve tracked Ayden down at her locker and told her about the tickets being five bucks a couple. "Yes?" Ayden said. "Did you get them?"

Steve looked down at the floor. "All tapped out," he murmured.

It took a while for Ayden to catch on that he didn't have enough cash on him. She gave him the money, hoping nobody was watching.

That Saturday, the day of the big dance, Ayden rushed home from shopping with her mom. She showered, fixed her hair, slipped into the cute outfit she'd just bought. She was getting more and more excited and could hardly stand it. This was her first dance at her new school. She felt like she was making her debut.

Going out to dinner with other couples before the dance was a tradition too. When she called Steve to see what time he was going to pick her up, she got his goofy voice on the answering machine. She figured he was still in the shower or something. Ayden called one of the girls and told her they should just go ahead—she and Steve would catch up with them later.

Seven o'clock came and Ayden was getting hungry. She started to wonder what kind of boy would make a girl wait this long without even calling. Ayden didn't know where Steve was, but she knew that he had ruined the night. Worse, he had ruined her standing at the new school.

At 9:43 P.M. the phone rang. It was Steve. Ayden doesn't remember exactly what she said to him, but she got the point across that she was livid. All Steve said to explain his not showing up was, "I just fell asleep on the couch, okay? Why didn't you call me? This is *all your fault*. Why's every girl always treating me like dirt?" That's when Ayden realized that a dorky, spur-of-the-moment, and way desperate date is *never* better than no date. And later, when she 'fessed up to her new friends, they apologized. "We shoulda told you he's a 'wince,' not a Prince," they said.

**Could You Be a
Flunky Magnet?**

1 The Flunky in your grade seems to have fallen for you. He follows you around like a shadow and picks up every pen you accidentally drop. You . . .

- **a.** Plan your day to completely avoid the Flunky. You figure out alternate routes to class every day, duck into the girls' room, and even get to school an hour early sometimes.
- **b.** Are, like, sooo thrilled that a boy is this into you. You walk slow so he can catch up to you between classes and then you wait for him to say or do something. So what if he majors in belching?
- **c.** Are so excited. You're going to make him over until he is perfect, even if he's not right for you. You make plans to buy him new clothes and teach him some manners.
- **d.** Let him know as kindly as you can that he's making you feel uncomfortable. Then go on with your fun life.

2 The Flunky in line behind you in the cafeteria starts talking to you. He is so gross everyone avoids him. You joke around with him because you're bored. Next thing you know, he sits Velcroed to your side at your table and stares at you. You . . .

- **a.** Get up quickly, dump your lunch in the trash, and run to the library to hide out in the stacks for the rest of lunch period.
- **b.** Bat your lashes and act coy. Even a Flunky's better than no boy to flirt with at all.
- **c.** Make sure he accompanies you to your next class, even if you have to sling him over your shoulder. This way the cool guy in fifth period will see what a hot chick you are.
- **d.** Realize that you made a mistake. Bolt your meal, dash to a club meeting you suddenly "remembered," and avoid standing in line next to this boy from now on.

3 Your best friend has started acting very different from her usual self. She has been hanging all over the Flunkies and when you tell her about it, she says, "You're just jealous." You . . .

a. Agree with her—it could be jealousy. All you know is that it makes you uncomfortable to see, so you avoid her from now on.

b. Decide she is seeing something in them that you're not see-ing. You practice all your flirtatious moves in the mirror at home and decide to try them out on some Flunkies of your own in school tomorrow.

c. Come right out and stake your claim. As soon as she gives attention to a Flunky, you go up to him and tell him he's so hot, right to his face.

d. Explain to her that flirting just to flirt could end up hurting her. If she doesn't listen to you, you may have to distance yourself from her. She's going to get a rep.

4 The weekend's coming up. Your buds all have boyfriends to take to the movie you're all seeing, and they are trying to fix you up with a Flunky. You . . .

a. Decide that your stomach and your head are hurting beyond belief. You might have the flu—what a good excuse not to go to the movies!

b. Listen to their advice and take the date with the Flunky. Your friends know what's best for you, and nobody ever promised you no growing pains.

c. Take the date with the Flunky and then flirt with all your friends' boys while you're at the flick.

d. Say, "No thanks." Instead, you get a group of other singles together and go bowling with them or grab a pizza.

Now it's time to find out your true Crush Quotient, your CQ. Tally your answers and find the description that best fits you. If you have a mixture, look at all the breakdowns. Obviously, there's a bit of everything in you, which is fab. Now, can you work on having a little less of the answer A attitude and a little more of the answer D attitude?

Mostly A's: Scared Sarah

It's time to put aside your hanky, baby blanket, and other signs of being sooo scared. What is it with you and boys? They're just human beings like you and your crew. And as for your buds, don't let them push you around so much!

Mostly B's: Eager Evelyn

Just because a Flunky takes an interest in you doesn't mean you have to return the feeling. You are a super girl and you own the world. So, of course, you attract all kinds of guys. It's up to you to weed out the bad boys from the rad boys.

Mostly C's: Rottweiler Renee

Dealing with boys—whether they're hunks or flunks—isn't a contest. So stop stressing about it and attacking every boy who looks your way. Just know that with your spunk, you can achieve anything. Figure out what types of boys are right for you. Then talk to one or two and become their friend first.

Mostly D's: Astounding Alexis

You get lots done and still manage to have fun. But even on boring days—and we all have those—getting entangled with a Flunky is never on your to-do list. You're just too self-confident and poised to "play" with lost-cause boys. Good for you!

FLUNKY FACTORS:
What Should You Know about the Flunky?

In every large group of boys, you will find one or two Flunkies. These boys aren't *bad* bad, but they're for sure way too immature for you.

> This one boy on the bus acts like he's about three years old. He sucks soda through straws that he sticks up his nose and does all kinds of other gross stuff. —Becky, 13

Yes, the Flunkies are several years behind in growing up, not physically but mentally and emotionally. They want attention desperately, and since they're not mature enough to get it through playing sports or excelling in a club, they get it any way they can.

This immaturity isn't something you or other girls can cure quickly. Sometimes, by the time he *graduates*, the Flunky can learn to act his age, have good manners, and care about his work, but it's not your job to teach him. You're too busy with your own growing up. Even teachers and counselors shake their heads over the fact that the Flunky refuses to take advice and clean up his act. He just doesn't want to be nice. He'd rather live on the fringes of the boy world than go with the rules, show school spirit, or care about others.

> My top secret: Take a close look at every boy you meet. If he's annoying, you won't enjoy being around him ever. Don't fool yourself and think you can give him a makeover. Even if you could, it would take years. By the time you realize your mistake, all the great guys are long gone. —Lissa, 16

The Flunky clusters around other Flunkies, and when they get together, oh, man! They smear mayo on the banister in the staircase; they put glue in the locks of teachers' rooms; they toilet-paper girls' houses. Worse for you, they hang out in hallways and make really loud, very crude remarks about girls walking by. They say nasty things about the girls' chests or behinds and the girls either get angry or embarrassed. If a teacher catches them, the Flunkies say they didn't do anything and didn't mean any harm. In their minds, they may think they're not hurting anyone. One thing's for sure, though, they are definitely hurting their standing in school.

There's this bunch of really annoying boys in my school that spend all their time getting on people's nerves. — Jodi, 14

Remember, just because a boy annoys you once doesn't necessarily mean he's a Flunky. It's the boys who act like jerks on purpose *all the time* that will set off that red-light warning.

It's a good thing that most everyone sees through Flunkies sooner or later. People may laugh at first when a Flunky falls down as he walks in late to class for the second time, but Flunkies are never popular for long. And years later, many of them are still where they were in school—nowhere. And any girls who hang with them don't end up achieving much either.

FLUNKY FIZZLERs:
What You Should Do about the Flunky

When you meet a boy whom almost nobody likes (duh, a Flunky), a boy who makes you feel uncomfortable and whom you just don't like, don't get caught in a conversation with him for too long.

If you act too friendly with a known Flunky, you will regret it. They tend to stick like Elmer's glue. — Rena, 17

So if the Flunky catches your eye or says hello, say a distracted "hey" but don't smile, and be on your way quickly. Flunkies can be so desperate, they'll latch on to even a hint of friendliness. It doesn't take much before you'll end up having to get some Flunky repellent going.

Don't *ever* let your desire to have a boyfriend cloud your eyes. Going out with a boy just because he asked and no one else did is *never* the solution. The solution is to zero in on someone worth your time, walk by his locker between classes and say "hi," and then see what happens. Would you pick out the yuckiest, barfy-est outfit in a store? No way! You try to find the nicest clothes, the ones you like the most. So why not treat boys with the same attitude and respect?

Don't believe the nobody-likes-me stories the Flunky enjoys telling any girl who will listen. Sure, there are definitely boys in school who have been bullied, and there are others who aren't popular for no apparent reason. But most boys do give other boys a chance. Really, only the most unpleasant and most immature boys end up totally alone (or hanging out with other rude and immature boys).

When you submit to Flunkies and talk to or flirt with them, or even sometimes go on dates with them, you're really just using them anyhow. Girl, you are *not* in the market for the strays. You have too much going for yourself to be suckered into hanging out with the losers and users in your school.

BOY STORY—A Real-Life Story from a Girl Like You

I had a mega crush on an awesome boy when I was in ninth grade, but the catch was that he was a senior and I knew that he wouldn't talk to me because I was too young. He didn't know I liked him. He didn't know I even *existed*. I was dying to go to the home-coming dance, just to be near him, look at him, figure out what songs he liked the most.

This yucky, sucky ninth-grade boy who I didn't like and who nobody else liked asked me to the dance. I wanted to see the senior of my dreams, so I said, "Sure, why not?" Maybe I would be able to get close to the senior, even stand next to him, you know? I day-dreamed about "accidentally" brushing my arm against his to start a conversation. I was so stoked I would be sharing the same space with him for a *whole* evening! I was going to look so pretty, there's no way he wouldn't know who I was at the end of the evening.

Man, did I super primp and go crazy making sure my outfit was perfect before this dance. Well, what a disappointment it turned out to be. Go figure, the senior of my dreams came for only twenty-three minutes and seventeen seconds with this college-looking beauty and I was stuck all evening with that lame ninth grader. You know what he did? Talked nonstop about his Lego toy collection and said that his life's dream was wiping up the spilled water and sweat and stuff off the floor at the b'ball games. And he used his sleeve as a Kleenex! Twice!

Debi, 14

Grade the Girls

Serves you right, Debi. You should never use a boy, even if he is an unlikable Flunky. It just isn't cool, and it earns you a D−. How would you like it if someone asked you out just so he could hang out and talk to your best friend? Wouldn't that make you feel terrible? Sure it would, so you don't ever want to make a boy (or anyone) feel terrible. Saying you had such a mega crush on someone that you couldn't resist going with a Flunky is not a good excuse.

Don't worry. You'll have a chance to redeem yourself. Next time a dud asks you out, kindly tell him the truth. Say, "Sorry, I can't, I'm not dating anyone right now." Or you can give the perfectly acceptable excuse that you're going with girlfriends because your parents said you couldn't date yet (or on that weekend). It may be the truth, or very close to it. But remember, if you say you're going with girlfriends or you're not going to the dance, you *can't* then go to the event with another boy—it's a big no-no. And then you may end up missing out on an opportunity to go with a Prince! So it's best to just stick with the truth and give a firm "No thanks" to the Flunky. The fact is, lying of any magnitude is still lying.

PRINCESS PROMOTERS:
Time for Academic Add-Justments

Many Flunkies skip school or club meetings or swim practice. As a consequence, they never reach their Prince potential—not even close. That's so opposite from the way you are. You want to be the best you can be.

1. So today, think about where you see yourself in five or ten years. What do you want to do with your life? Which would you rather be someday—a veterinarian, librarian, baker, jewelry designer, or teacher?

2. OK, now it's time to give your big dreams a reality check by seeing your guidance counselor and asking him or her if you're on track academically for a super future. Be ready to tell the counselor what you see yourself doing. See what advice you'll get to reach that goal. Are you doing great, grade- and course-wise?

3. Back at home in your room, put awards and trophies in a more prominent place and add-just your space to highlight your academic plans. Pull out your best essay or your top science test and put them up on your bulletin board or on the wall. Cut out magazine pictures of women (and men) you admire and put them up to inspire you to reach higher. Spend a few minutes adding a little something to your life to make you feel wonderful about yourself. Here's another little thing to do just for you: Go through this morning's paper and look for a story of somebody doing something nice, something special. It can be anything from saving a starving kitten to making bookmarks for some nursing homers. Get a clue and plan some little something similar that you—yes, you—can do.

    And then get it done—what fun.

Boy Secrets

Flunkies usually know exactly how annoying they are, but they don't care about changing. Change means they'd actually have to do something, to put effort into something, but they're so lazy they won't do it.

> Flirting is a very confusing thing to me. I know the general idea behind it——letting the other person know you like her. But I don't really know how to do it and I really don't care to impress some silly old girls. ——Richie, 14

This is one of the Flunky's problems: He doesn't care about girls, and he even has a negative attitude about girls.

Basically, he either doesn't want girls' attention or he's so desperate for attention he will pull flat-out dumb stunts to get it.

> I was trying to flirt with this girl but I was in such a rush that I didn't realize my fly was down. She thought I did it on purpose and got mad. I liked that, so now I know how to get attention from her. ——Bernie, 14

Some girls think they're being nice when they talk to Flunkies, but they don't realize that a lot of Flunkies actually look down on girls. And if a girl maybe doesn't feel that great about herself and gets excited when a guy, even a Flunky, talks to her, that just reinforces what the Flunky thinks.

> Some girls are way easy to fool. All you gotta do is get their attention. Be a doofus, be nasty, whatever, and they act like you are with the Prize Patrol. ——Farrell, 17

Boy File

Get out your Boy File! Take some of the cards and head them "Flunkies." Then write down the names of the totally unacceptable guys in your school, using the familiar Crush Code. Under each code name, write what makes this guy so objectionable.

Then on the back of the cards, write down the opposite qualities. For example, if Flunky #1 dresses real sloppy, write down the opposite—"Neat dresser." Or if he always talks with food prominently displayed in his mouth, write down: "Good table manners" or "Eating politely." Do this until you've made a list of all the *positive* behaviors that the Flunkies would have to adopt (without any encouragement from you) to get them off your Flunky list.

On another note card, make the heading "Flunky Warning Signs" and copy over the list of negative stuff they do and say. Figure out the ten worst things a boy can do around you to make you consider him a total Flunky Frog. Here are some examples from girls your age.

What makes me go "yuck" is any boy who gives me the creeps.
—Jordan, 13

Boys who make you feel uncomfortable or who just seem bad should be avoided.

Any boy who says "hi" to me a million times a day with a big grin on his face and his tongue hanging out is somebody I'm so not interested in. —LeAnn, 15

Acting inappropriately all the time is a Flunky warning sign.

My secret is to check out a guy's buds. If they're all, like, cavemen—you know, real gross guys—I make myself scarce. Who needs to be grossed out? Not me. —Beth, 14

Ask your friends who they think the Flunkies are in your school, and why. Swear to each other that you'll always tell one another if you suspect one is about to get involved with a Flunky.

Final Exam

So how does the Flunky stack up? Take a look at page 33 in Chapter 3 for the report card breakdown info.

The Flunky's Report Card

Looks: F, not always, but most of the time
Schoolwork: F, in most every subject
Attitude: P (let's just give him the benefit of the doubt, okay?)
Behavior: F
Activities: F, not always, but most of the time

Added up, that means the Flunky gets 4 F's. That puts his Prince-for-you potential in the pitiful category. It's much better for you if you stay away from the Flunkies. Even if you think there's a sweet guy underneath the Flunky outside, there's no reason to deal with his nonsense just to find out. You're way better off concentrating on the many great boys out there.

CHAPTER 7

The Toady

The second type of bogus boy is the Toady. Often, the Toady looks good and you may think he is super crush-worthy. He may have his act together schoolwise and play sports. Plus, he may even have a nice allowance. But there's just something *wrong* with him. You can't put your finger on it, but something inside you tells you he just isn't right for you. The dictionary defines a *toady* as a "flatterer and repulsive person." It's too bad the Toady doesn't come across as repulsive when you first meet him. He's a smooth talker and ever so likable, so nice—almost too nice, really. After a while, you'll see through his front and realize what he really is: a Toady. Ever heard the expression "He thinks he's God's gift to women"? Yep, you guessed it, that's the Toady!

Don't judge a guy only by his pearly whites or cool duds—or his wad of cash. —Jessica, 16

Unlike the dirty Flunky, the Toady doesn't forget to shower. He wears stylish clothes, and when he gets to high school, he drives a cool car. He even comes across as a hottie and has plenty of friends. But underneath, he may have a big problem—a problem that can spill over on you.

Bad boys can come in the most gorgeous packages ever designed by the Maker, but inside they're up to nothing good. —Juli, 15

BOY WATCH:
What Makes a Boy a Toady?

When you first met Mike, he talked to you like he only had eyes for you. Then the next day, you realized he was doing the same thing to your best friend. You watched a little closer and saw Mike flirting with every girl in your grade. Mike isn't interested in you, no matter what he says. He's interested in only himself and in how to make himself look good. That's why he wants all the girls. Mike acts like he was born to flirt with girls. He says anything to make girls like him. He uses them and lies to them because Mike doesn't think girls are his equals. The worst part is that Mike gets away with it because he's cute and dresses in good clothes. A lot of girls forgive him when he lies, stands them up, or cheats on them. But you know he's a Toady and you see right through him—good job, girl!

If you could get into Mike's head for a day, you'd see what his biggest problem is: Mike, confident as he may seem, has low self-esteem. To make himself feel better and super macho, he collects female admirers like you collect purses. Mike isn't a Toady because he is a horrible person. It's that his parents are Toadies themselves, and he got the wrong ideas from them. His parents are big hypocrites and there were rumors that his dad cheated on his mom.

Mike, like other Toadies, is smart and clever, but he is so mixed up about girls. You've noticed Mike can size up any girl and zoom in on her weak spots to make her feel bad. If he notices a girl has skinny legs or a few pimples, he'll call attention to it—not flat-out mean but slyly. And he's not sparing in his dissing of girls either. Oh no. He can target any chick that, in his opinion, doesn't make him look or has the nerve to reject his advances. This is called passive aggressiveness, and it's one of the big trademarks of a Toady.

Dear Dr. Erika:

There is this boy at school who always comes up to me and whispers stuff in my ear, like, "Man, you look hot today." I can't even get away from him 'cause he stays right with me. He's never loud, only soft-spoken, but he's always there. Maybe he has spies all over, but wherever I go, there he is, saying sexy things to me that make my face turn beet red. My friend, Emily, said he does the same thing to her, too!

Mallory, 15

Dear Dr. Erika:

Last week my friend Liz invited me to a party at her house. When I got there, no one had arrived yet. Liz was busy in the kitchen getting the snacks. So I wandered around and then I saw this boy Liz likes. He's supposed to be her boyfriend. Anyway, he started talking to me, and he, like, cornered me. The next day at school he told everybody I was his new hot girlfriend. He was, like, bragging about it, but I'm so not his girlfriend. I don't even like him—yuck!

Liana, 16

Sounds as if both girls are dealing with the Toady. The Toady is out for only his own gain. But once you unmask him in all his various disguises, you're up to the task.

FYI

The one thing about the different kinds of Toadies is that the Toady is always an untrustworthy boy. You'll find that he comes in three categories.

The Muscle Macho

This is a boy who strolls down the hall with his friends, looking pumped up and leaving no room for anyone else to get through. The Muscle Macho acts like a bulldozer. He is fully aware of crowding other people out. What he's hoping for is to run into some girls who'll be awed by his hot body.

My secret? I wear a short-sleeved shirt that shows off my biceps—all it takes to get some girls to act very friendly.
—Jonathan, 15

Ew, Jonathan! The girls are probably just trying to squeeze past the Muscle Macho, but he assumes they are after him. That's what he wants—a little physical contact with girls. He's never a real threat but is way inconsiderate and way too into himself.

The Hall and Mall Crawlers

You've definitely seen these boys. They spend their free time wandering around any area where girls congregate. These boys zero in on groups of girls to trail, and they yell things and say things to make contact with one of them. They act like stalkers! Instead of checking out the wares at Target, they target a girl's pretty hair, nice legs, or other body parts. The more girls they can add to their Buddy Lists, the better. And, of course, they brag about their many conquests.

The Roam-eo

This is a Toady who's *always* on the lookout for the next girl. Even before he breaks up with his latest girlfriend, he's got a new one waiting. You can tell if Romeo is a real Roam-eo by looking at his eyes while he talks to you. If his eyes are always roaming while he's supposed to be having a convo with you, you know he's probably scouting around for his next best female bud.

Watch out for boys who check out the waitress at IHOP while they're having lunch with you. Never a good sign if their eyes are everywhere but on you. —Tamara, 16

True. For the Roam-eo, any new chick is always dreamier than the one he's with at the moment.

Universal High School

The one time Sherry thought she was really, truly, finally in love was at the end of sophomore year. His name was Jay. She thought he was the sweetest, most caring guy she'd ever met. She loved everything about him: his beautiful skin, his style, his walk, and most of all, his considerate personality. She looked forward to going to church so she could see him. The things he said are what made her *really* fall for him. His lines were so smooth: "Your smile is so beautiful," "You blow my mind," "I don't want to come on too strong, but I'm really serious about you. . . . I will always, *always* love you." And all this after he'd just met her! They talked every day and spent hours together at the mall and going to movies.

Then came band camp, a three-week statewide summer camp at Universal High that Sherry so looked forward to every year. Sherry put up pictures of Jay and her everywhere—in her band locker, crammed into her purse, and tucked inside her instrument case.

Sherry couldn't wait for the other band campers to ask her about the hot boy in all the photos. She could hear herself bragging about him. DeAndra, a friend of Sherry's best friend, noticed the pictures first. Sherry knew that DeAndra never liked her. DeAndra studied the pictures of Sherry and Jay and commented sharply, "Oh, so you know Jay. Do you know Jennifer?"

"No," Sherry replied with wide eyes, a little bit worried.

"That's Jay's girlfriend. They've been dating for two years."

"Are you for real?" Sherry asked with tears in her voice.

"Yes, and they were talking for about six months before they actually started dating," DeAndra said, satisfied that she had delivered the worst news of Sherry's life.

Sherry left the room and went to the bathroom, where she cried for half an hour. She cried so hard, she became light-headed.

She went back to her locker and put on some sunglasses to hide her red and puffy eyes.

She skipped out on breakfast and went home. In her room, she ran around yelling like a mad woman, wondering why this had to happen and cursing Jay. She tore up every picture of herself and Jay and cried some more.

She decided to call him and make sure DeAndra hadn't been lying. Holding back her tears, she confronted him with what DeAndra had told her. He denied everything, said it was all a lie, and insisted on coming over the next day to spend time with her back at band camp.

She was in the band room with her friends when she saw his convertible pull up. She walked outside, deep in conversation with her friends. She wanted to act like she didn't see him, to see what he would do. Jay came up behind her and gave her a hug and a big hello. She instantly felt like she'd been wrong. This was Jay, the most popular graduate of Universal High, acting like his old self, saying all the cool words, and falling all over himself to be nice to Sherry.

She was floating on a cloud. Later, she returned from a band meeting and overheard several campers talking about seeing Jay. "Yeah, he was visiting Sherry, but he said he came here to see Jennifer and then he's planning to see Suzanne. . . ."

It was all over then. Sherry cried every day for a week. In the end, she decided that her experience with Jay was both a curse and actually a *gift*, too. Sure, she got hurt badly and felt embarrassed, but the gift was that she had learned a valuable lesson: When a guy seems too good to be true, he often is (a Toady!).

Could You Be a Toady Magnet?

 Your school has a Wall of Toadies, with a few Flunkies thrown in for good measure. During lunch, they lean against the wall and shout out their ratings of any passing girl's body parts. You . . .

a. Wear a baggy fleece top or tie an extra shirt around your waist to cover your curves. Then you either avoid the wall or walk past it *real* fast.

b. Listen to your ratings and remember them. Like, last week, these guys gave you only a 5 on your midriff. So this week, you're not eating any desserts.

c. Wear a low-cut shirt or some tight pants and make sure you swing your hips as you walk by. You got the highest rating last week and you want to keep it that way.

d. Tell your teachers about it and write an article titled "The Wall of Shame" for the school paper. You can handle the degrading remarks but you're not going to allow these losers to lower the self-esteem of other girls.

 You have a crush on a boy, so you're going to the movies with him, your best friend, and her crush. During the previews, you and your best friend's crush go to get the popcorn and drinks. When you come back, you spot your best friend holding hands with your crush, and he's even got his other hand on her leg! You . . .

a. Sneak back out to the lobby quietly. You're hurt but you don't really want to make a scene. You figure you'll just pretend it never happened but you know you'll be crying yourself to sleep tonight.

b. Say "ahem" so they notice you're back and stop. The movie's about to start and you don't want to miss it. Your crush is too cute to get mad at, and your best friend is so cool. You'll just be sure to flirt extra-hard with her crush.

c. Dump the popcorn on your crush's head, "accidentally" drop the soda into your best friend's purse, and stomp out of the theater, yelling about their dirty, jerky selves and how you'll never talk to either of them again.

d. Pause for a moment and try to calm down, even though your heart is thumping in your ears. You feel like your best friend has betrayed you and now you know your crush is actually a sleazeball. For the time being, if this is a great movie, you sit somewhere else and enjoy what you paid for. If it's just so-so, you leave. You'll deal with each of them later.

3 This Toady you run into every day before history class always bars your way. When you try to get around him, he grins and touches your neck or shoulder, wherever. He makes you feel sooo uncomfortable. And he says stuff under his breath to you, too. You . . .

a. Just put up with it and try not to dread history class every day. It could be worse. He could be actually grabbing you or trying to kiss you.

b. Giggle and bat your eyelashes whenever he gets close. It's so cool that guys can't keep their hands off of you.

c. Touch him back and say sweet things back to him. And you won't quit until he begs for mercy.

d. Tell him to leave you alone, now. If he doesn't, you whip out a note card and write down what he's doing, when, and where and threaten that the card will be turned in anonymously. And, if he keeps it up, you personally report him to a teacher.

4 This Toady is always after you, trying to flatter you, even though his presence is constantly unwanted. Everybody knows that he does the same thing to other girls. He practically camps out by the office to get first dibs on new girls, and they usually fall for it because he is so cute. It's customary to attend the end-of-the-year picnic as a couple, and the Toady has asked you to go with him. You . . .

a. Wonder what you did wrong. Even though you've never been receptive to his advances, did you maybe encourage him in some way? You think about the clothes you've worn in front of him or if you've ever smiled in his direction. It makes you sick to even think he thinks you could be interested.

b. Feel very grateful someone has asked you. You spend some time picking out a hot outfit and making some food to bring.

c. Find out what the Toady's planning on wearing and then coordinate your outfit to match his. You even buy the same kind of chain he wears so your jewelry will match.

d. Tell him, "No thanks, I'm going with my girls." Even though you'd like to go, you'd never even think of going with him! The Toady's hard to shake now, so if you went to the picnic with him, you might be stuck with him forever.

> Now it's time to find out your true Crush Quotient, your CQ. Tally your answers and find the description that best fits you. If you have a mixture, look at all the breakdowns. Obviously, there's a bit of everything in you, which is fab. Now, can you work on having a little less of the answer A attitude and a little more of the answer D attitude?

Mostly A's: Tearful Tara
You have such a kind heart, now you must take heart. Don't flee from any boys, no matter how scared you are of them. They're just students like you. Put them in their place if they need it. And don't always think you did something wrong when some boys come on too strong.

Mostly B's: Overwhelmed Oriana
Don't be freaked out whenever a boy takes notice of you—especially if he's not a bad one. Just stay cool, size up the situation, then make moves that are well thought-out. Boys don't rule your life, so be in charge. Your wishes matter, not theirs.

Mostly C's: Combative Connie

Sure, the bad guys should be stopped, but often that's best done with a cool plan, not a clumsy pounce on them. Use your energy to concentrate on other things—like yourself! Back off from boys, whether you like them or not.

Mostly D's: Clear-Headed Claire

You keep a cool head even when some of the boys in your world turn out to be anti-Princes. If some of those boys happen to be nice guys, great. If not, you still have all your fab friends to spend time with till you do find a Prince someday.

TOADY FACTORS:
What Should You Know about the Toady?

One of the things all Toadies have in common is that they pay lots of attention to their looks. They work out a lot and gel their hair so much it feels like plastic. They smell like an aftershave commercial and pay more attention to their clothing than you do.

> Watch out for any boys who look in the mirror more than you do. They're incapable of liking you cause they're already taken— by and with themselves. —Monica, 14

The Toady's self-absorption is not the biggest worry. And you don't need to care about his bling or his style. It's what's going on inside his mind that you should be wary of. His values are not straight and the Toady can never be trusted to tell the truth, to treat you right, and to respect girls.

> I think a sense of honor is the most important trait in a boy. He's got to have it. —Julissa, 15

That's why Toadies are problem boys. They don't have any sense of honor when it comes to girls. They say anything to get what they want. They're just so self-centered that their own wishes take priority over everything. Toadies consider boys to be superior to girls. They think girls should be grateful if the Toadies give them some attention.

Some Toadies even specialize. They go after girls who maybe have some weak spots. Maybe a girl hasn't ever gotten a lot of attention, or maybe everyone knows she feels bad about being a little overweight. The Toady might target her so he can feel better about himself and brag to his posse about having another girl on the line.

TOADY FIZZLERS:
What You Should Do about the Toady

Anytime you meet a smooth-talking boy who seems to be overly interested in his appearance, step back and ask yourself, is this just a nice-looking gift box with nothing inside? It's always a good idea to ask other girls about him. They'll clue you in on potential Toadies.

I warn my friends about any dude who's no good. —Rita, 15

Once you have determined that a boy is a Toady, keep him on the friend level, the *distant*-friend level, that is, and nothing more. Don't just *like* like him because he's around and tells you that you're cute, like, every day.

My best friend is in love with getting infatuated. Every other boy she sees in the hall, she's like, "Oh, oh, he's sooo cute." She keeps obsessing over him even though she doesn't know him and wouldn't even want to know him. I mean, it's way obvious—these boys she picks to like are trouble. —Justine, 15

Boys with a rep for being no good, who everyone knows kissed so-and-so last weekend even though he's with someone else, must be off-limits to you. To crush seriously on a Toady is to go looking for trouble. How many Frogs have you ever heard about that turned into actual Princes? You can do better, girl, and you know it.

In short, the Toady uses girls to boost his ego. To him, just about any girl will do. He has picked up on some signs that tell him some girls are more open to his extreme flattery and advances. But even if you give off no signs, sometimes the Toady will pick you.

This I know for sure: When you dress, like, slutty, you can't expect to attract the nice guys. —Nancy, 15

So don't dress like Christina Aguilera for school, even if you love her music. Wear your own style and flair, but don't invite any Toadies into your life by sending the wrong message. They're way hard to get rid off.

BOY STORY—A Real-Life Story from a Girl Like You

I was remembering the other night how this boy and I used to say words like "forever" and "love," but it turned out everything was one-sided—and all the good stuff was coming from me.

All my friends, and even my mom, warned me about this boy from day one, but I wouldn't listen to any of them. They said he wasn't for real, but I blew them off. This boy I thought I knew, whom I thought I loved—he had another girlfriend on the side. He had been with her for a long time and said all the same things to her that he said to me. I could never look into the eyes of someone and tell them "I love you" if I was harboring a secret.

So now? Now I'm through with boys. I don't even want to look at any of those creeps, no matter how hard my friends try to get me to be sociable again. I feel like I'll never be able to trust another guy.

Caroline, 16

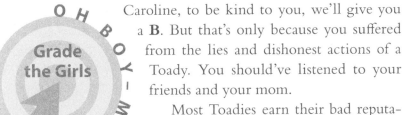

Caroline, to be kind to you, we'll give you a **B**. But that's only because you suffered from the lies and dishonest actions of a Toady. You should've listened to your friends and your mom.

Most Toadies earn their bad reputation the old-fashioned way—by treating girls badly. They usually leave a trail of disappointed girls behind them, each one thinking that maybe she could change this boy from unreliable to reliable, from promise breaker to promise keeper.

There are so many boys out there just waiting for you to say "hi." Don't take a chance on a Toady. You can feel bad about what happened from your run-in with a Toady, but you can't let that sour your entire experience in the wide world of boys! Caroline, your next step is to re-enter that world, keeping an eye out for the Frogs, especially the Toadies. This time, do what your friends advise. They have your best interests in mind. Write off that Toady and go on with your life!

PRINCESS PROMOTERS: *Time for Some Artistic Add-Justments*

To increase your Princess qualities, just take a couple of minutes here and there to honor your creative side. You know you're loaded with all kinds of talents, but often you're just in a rush to keep up with your routine. You've got tons of emotions pent up, just waiting to be expressed.

> Great guys are drawn to girls that stand out in some way. Maybe a cool guy will take notice of you when you're in the drama club or the choir, or when the school hangs up the photo you took. —Claudia Lee, 14

1. Even if you carry a tune about as well as a sieve holds water, you can still express yourself through your voice. Make up any kind of song and sing it, loud. Or take a top tune and come up with new words for it and sing that. Or write two or three lines of words that express the way you feel, then hum them along to a cool tune.

2. Get out a sheet of paper and doodle something. Don't even think about what you're drawing, just sketch whatever flows from your head. Color the result with markers or pencils. Or, cut out a few pictures from your fave mags and glue them down collage-style on a piece of poster board. Let your creative nature direct you.

3. On another day, pull out all your old shirts, skirts, scarves, and jeans that aren't good enough to donate to Goodwill or pass down to a sister or relative. Cut out cloth squares and arrange them to your liking on a flat surface, any way you wish. Then, stitch them together patchwork-style to make a mini-quilt. You've just made a memory quilt of the old outfits you used to wear!

Boy Secrets

How do the Toadies regard girls? It's a shame: Most Toadies aren't the least bit ashamed of the dishonorable ways they treat girls.

> I really like messing with girls' heads, flirting with lots of them and telling each the same hot lines, and then watching the fallout. It's a game to me and I play it with any girl dumb enough to go along. —Barton, 16

Some Toadies go beyond not being ashamed. They actually *brag* about how many girls they can "get." The Toadies try to convince a bunch of girls from various schools and neighborhoods that they really *like* like each girl.

Watch out for any guys that all of a sudden tell you they're in love with you. They may not even like you. It's just a phony thing guys do to show off in front of each other. Makes them feel like they are marking off their territory—like, "Hey, these chicks are mine. See how easy I can get 'em?" —Sherman, 15

And still other Toadies make a science out of duping girls. They keep score of how many girls each day listened to the syrupy flattery and insincere declarations of devotion without laughing in the Toadies' faces.

I have this book where I mark down how long it takes me to sweet-talk a girl before she follows me around like a puppy. The longest time, three days, and the shortest, four minutes. —Beau, 17

Don't be fooled easily by the Toadies around you. They may look hot, but inside, they're so not.

My top secret? You gotta learn to ditch the dishonest guys fast. Never be taken in by their cool talking and their machismo. —Kaelin, 16

Boy File

Grab a few blank file cards and head each of them up "Toady." Use your Crush Code to list the boys you know who belong in that category. What boys in your school collect girls like baseball cards and CDs? What boys are always passing out insincere compliments? Has any boy ever acted Toady-like toward you? Are there any Muscle Machos in your school? Have you ever run across any Hall and Mall Crawlers who followed you around? Are there any Roam-eos in your world? Write down what red flags you have noticed that announce so clearly these boys are not to be trusted.

Then turn the cards over and write down the sincere ways that boys can show interest in girls.

Enlist the help of your best friends to talk about some of the not-so-nice boys you know.

Always remember this rule (in fact, write it down on a card!): If you have a bad feeling about a boy (or hear something bad about him), go with your gut. A long time ago, before humans formed civilizations, our instincts were what kept us safe. So when you feel turned off by a boy, or when you hear something about him that turns you off, and it's something way factual, and not just some rumor, pay attention to those feelings and realize he's a Toady. Girl, you need to be confident and self-assured in everything you do. Be most concerned with your own life—never mind obsessing over boys. Most of them aren't Toadies, but boys will be around when the time is right. You don't need to do anything to get boys' interests, just be yourself.

Final Exam

So how does the Toady stack up? Take a look at page 33 in Chapter 3 for the report card breakdown info.

The Toady's Report Card

Looks: P, though not always
Schoolwork: P, though not every subject
Attitude: F minus minus
Behavior: F minus minus
Activities: P, though not always

Added up, that means the Toady gets 3 F's—more, actually, because the double minuses add up to another F. That puts his Prince-for-you potential at poor or even pitiful. The Toady is a frog, no matter how you look at it.

CHAPTER 8

The Bad Boy, aka the Jerk or the Punk

The third and last type of bogus boy you need to watch out for is the boy who *enjoys* causing trouble. When he's given a choice, he prefers to do something that seriously disturbs or hurts someone else, and not just girls. These boys are just—for lack of a better word—*bad*. They believe they can do whatever they want and get away with it. They are blatant abusers of rules and school policies, and breakers of other people's trust and of girls' hearts. And worse.

> If you go out with a troublemaker, you'll get in trouble faster than you can say <u>uno</u>, <u>dos</u>, <u>tres</u>. So don't even think about it. —Miriam, 15

For all these reasons, it's important to be wary of Bad Boys. Of all the Frogs, they are the worst: They are the poisonous frogs. They don't appear in big numbers. But in every grade level in whatever school, you'll find one or even a few.

> You know what? Suicide is what can happen to you if you fall in love with a bad guy and find out he's been lying to you, cheating on you, and trashing you every way he could. That scum, he made my best friend want to die, but I saved her. —Maria Anna, 16

Now listen. This is most important. If you find yourself getting caught up way deep in the drama of Bad Boys and bad relationships—or if one of your friends is—you need to act fast. Don't wait—call or e-mail your guidance counselor right away. Or make an appointment to see him or her first thing tomorrow morning. That's what the guidance counselor is there for! You can also call a suicide hotline number. Go to http://suicidehotlines. com or call 1–800-SUICIDE or 1–800-784-2233. And don't ever think that you might be bothering these people. That's what they get paid for—they're here for your friends and for you, okay? They want to help—please, give them a chance.

BOY WATCH:
What Makes a Boy a Bad Boy?

Darryl comes from a chaotic home. His mom shows up now and then to pick up some clean clothes for herself. His dad calls before he comes home to see if Mom's gone. Only then does he drop by to leave some cash on the kitchen table that is piled high with dirty dishes. It's never enough to pay the bills, so sometimes the power is out. Gramma rushes in when she can to get things back on track, and even leaves some stew in the fridge.

Darryl's older brother moved out last year. Nobody knows where to, but it means Darryl and his crew pretty much have the whole place to themselves now. They party whenever they want to, and on days when nothing's happening, they drag to school.

Darryl sometimes wishes he could have regular folks like a few of the other dudes he hangs with. But then that would cramp his style, and nobody better do that to him. He just turned fourteen but looks and acts older. Fending for yourself since age eleven can do that to you.

Darryl, like most Bad Boys, wasn't born bad. He became "bad" because nobody is there for him. He's never had a solid role model. Darryl's parents, either on purpose or unknowingly, helped make their kids into bad kids by not having rules and consequences, by covering up for whatever the kids did, by always excusing their bad behavior, by introducing them to adult topics too early, by breaking the law themselves, and by teaching them that *anger* is a good thing.

There are so many paths some parents take to reduce a good boy's potential, make him less than his best. They belittle him, push him around, never teach him respect and hard work, and never show him love. So sure, we feel for the Bad Boys like Darryl because their lives are tough, but that's *not your fault*. You know better than to welcome Darryl with open arms. He's a Bad Boy and you're smart to leave him alone.

Dear Dr. Erika:

My best bud is, like, crazy in love with this guy who is super-bad news. He broke into the drink machine at school and even took a teacher's car for a ride when the teacher left the key in it. But my friend won't listen to me when I tell her to quit going so crazy over such a loser. She's doing everything she can to impress him. She's, like, changed her appearance. She listens to different music now. She's even said that she would try bad substances if that's what the boy wants her to do.

Sunny, 14

Dear Dr. Erika:

My parents won't let me see this boy who lives two houses down, and they won't tell me why. Just "No, no, no!" is all they ever say. Whenever my parents think I can't hear them, they gossip about this boy's vandalizing mailboxes or some old busybody having seen him go through other folks' trash. They say he looks for paper and stuff so he can help this group of older kids who steal people's identities. But what's that got to do with me? This boy treats me sooo nice. Yesterday, he gave me a cell phone!

Dana, 15

Sounds as if both Sunny and Dana are talking about the Bad Boy. There is someone out there to make these boys better, but that's so not you. Sunny, it'd be smart for you to tell an adult what is going on with your friend. Make sure you don't let her drag you into anything. Dana, you need to learn to I-dentify the Bad Boys, I-solate them away from you, and I-nvest your time on good boys. Notice the capital *I*'s? That means, always, always think of what's best for you—say out loud, "*I* matter!"—and then proceed. Your parents are right: This boy is no good. He may have given you a cell phone, but that doesn't mean anything. No one can buy your attention and affection, girl! C'mon, it's time to ditch this Bad Boy and find yourself someone who's more Princely.

F y I

Some Bad Boys can often be identified from far away because their awful rep precedes them. Some drop out of school as soon as it's either legal or when the attendance officer gets tired of chasing them down. It's easy to avoid these obvious Bad Boys. But some bad guys cover up really well and act like super-great guys. They dress nice, talk nice, look way cute, and try to at least pass a few of their classes so they can continue to stay in school. In short, they pretend to be regular good guys.

They are *not* good guys though, and you can learn to identify these three groups of especially worrisome boys.

The Belittlers

These boys may be bright. They may be scrubbed so clean they squeak. But deep down, they feel like trash and want you to feel similarly. So they spend their time criticizing girls nonstop. Nothing the girl ever does will be good enough. Usually, this type of boy turned out not nice because he was constantly and harshly belittled by an older sib or an adult when he was a little kid. Inside, the Belittler feels stupid or dirty or just no #@*! good—no matter what the reality is. And he'll drag you down with him.

The Control Freak

The Control Freak will tell you what to do, what to wear, and what to eat. He takes over your life like a puppeteer, and you are the puppet. Not for long though—with a boy like this in your life, you'll soon become a broken doll. And he will blame you! This type of boy felt abandoned and helpless as a child. There was never anything or anyone he could count on. So now he desperately wants to control something—and that something is *you*.

> When I smack my girlfriend, it's never because of me; it's because she has disobeyed me. —Geoffrey, 18

That's scary. Geoffrey is just the type of Bad Boy you should watch out for. Remember, it is *never*, ever OK for a boy to hit a girl or vice versa.

The Mad Guys

This type of Bad Boy is always *angry*. He hates other people, hates his life, hates school, and basically hates whatever's in front of him. He is destructive toward himself and toward others.

> These scary guys in my school rip sinks off the wall in the bathroom, start fires in trash cans, and slash tires. And then they're like, "You chicks wanna come over this weekend?" I don't know where they want us to go, but my friends and I always act like we don't hear them. —Lucy, 15

Good job, Lucy. Ignoring the Bad Boys is a good thing. If you overhear someone planning an act of vandalism, it's your responsibility to let a teacher or someone else in charge know (and you can even do it anonymously, if you prefer).

Some of these Bad Boys exaggerate their anger, but others are really, actually mad. They go around and do crazy stuff, deep down hoping somebody will stop or catch them. You can't stop them, but there are professionals in your school who are the perfect people for the job. Your job is to let teachers or guidance counselors know when you notice boys who are being sadistic. If a boy is picking on a younger kid or kids repeatedly and in a really mean way, don't turn your back on the situation. If a boy is doing something destructive to the school or to himself, you don't need to overlook that. There are instances where it's totally OK to report a guy for something.

Of course, you don't want to run screaming to the office every time an older boy says something to a younger one. There are occasions when teasing younger kids can be good-natured and harmless. And here's how you can tell: Look at the face of the younger kid, the teasee. If he's beaming with joy or breaking into a grin or letting out a laugh, the teasing is probably acceptable. But if the teasee frowns, gets hurt, or slinks off in silence, then the teasing was probably unacceptable. As an added test, pretend what was said or done to the teasee was said or done to you. How do you feel? You'll know right away if the comment or action was warm, cheery, or joking.

One more thing: Bad Boys appear two ways—either as loners or as pack runners. The loners are brooders and they tend to have dark moods, like, every day. They hardly ever smile, and when they do, it doesn't reach their eyes. The pack runners find a band of Bad Boys who feel similar, and they always hang with a gang.

Universal High School

On Monday morning, in second-period English class, the teacher had a sore throat and couldn't lecture like she'd planned to. She gave the kids an assignment, to pick any topic to write about, as long as it had a message or a lesson. Kate read the assignment, opened her notebook, and grabbed a pencil. She waited for a moment, her forehead creased in a frown, and the story came pouring out.

Why did this have to happen to me? One day last year when I missed my ride after softball practice, a boy I kinda knew offered me a ride home. I'd seen him from the distance roaming the halls now and then but never talked to him. He didn't act like the other guys; he seemed above it all. When a teacher told him to report to class, he shrugged and went the other way. So I knew he wasn't, like, on the honor roll. He hardly ever came to school. Anyway, I accepted the ride and kept my cell in my hand the whole time, so I knew nothing could happen to me.

Well, something did happen—we hit it off. He asked me all kinds of things about myself, like he really cared. He seemed way nice. He would wait for me two or three times a week when I got to school and we kept talking, which led to going to get pizza and to the movies.

Luke and I quickly found ourselves tangled in the massive web that high school love can produce. It's the kind of web that completely surrounds young couples, shutting out the light from the outside world, leaving just the two

of you wrapped tightly in a warm but often <u>suffocating</u>

cocoon. Luke and I were happy together in the little world

we'd created. We had a few arguments, but they were

always over silly, trivial things.

In the fourth month of our relationship, I felt the need

to stretch and see what was happening in the rest of the

world. Although asking for more time to spend with my

neglected friends or on my science homework didn't seem

that demanding from my point of view, this request ignited

a dangerous flame in Luke. Luke made fun of my friends

and forbade me to see any of them, and he told me that

homework was a waste of time. He became a very control-

ling, demanding, dominant figure as I became his doormat.

It all came to a big, dramatic conclusion one Satur-

day. I arrived at Luke's home an hour later than planned

that afternoon. A mountain of chores and procrastinated

assignments had formed, and my parents were unwilling

to allow me to share the day with Luke before that mountain was reduced to a small mound. Luke's mom met me at the side door and whispered nervously, "<u>Psst,</u> watch out, Luke's having a bad day." <u>He's not the only one</u>, I thought, my body aching from all the work I'd done and my mind spinning from reading six nasty science chapters. Luke was lounging on the front porch. Although I'd told him that I'd be late, Luke still acted all cold when I got there.

"Hi, sorry I'm running late," I chirped, glad to see him but wondering why he wasn't dressed. We'd mentioned going out to an early dinner. I moved closer to give him a little hello kiss. He violently jerked his face away from me. "What's wrong?" I asked.

"Go home," he snapped. "Just leave, okay? It's too late to go to the lake now."

Nobody had even mentioned going to the lake, but I didn't point that out. Instead, I turned quickly and started toward my car. Luke had told me to leave several times before, but this was the first time I was actually going to

do it. So, with tears streaming down my cheeks, I slumped

down into my Honda and jammed the key into the ignition.

Before I could pull the car door completely closed, it swung

open forcefully and a strong arm reached in. Luke yanked

the key from the ignition and tossed it into the field that

touched his side yard. Luke ripped me out of the car next

and stood over me like an angry giant as he shoved me

hard against the car. He grabbed both of my forearms

so hard. "Listen to me," he said menacingly, "nobody—

nobody—disrespects me. Ever!"

"But I didn't—"

"You'd better apologize," he demanded. "Right now."

"For what?" I asked, struggling to break free from

his painful grasp.

"For making me mad!" he screamed. "It's all your

fault, all your fault." He stared at me, his eyes full of

hate. Luke's mom saw what was going on and sprinted to

where he held me against the car. She shouted at him to let

me loose, a good thing because my arms were getting numb.

And I was so scared. Luke's mother had to slap him on the

cheek several times before he finally let go. I ran to the field

and started frantically looking for my keys. Then I heard

Luke's enraged mother yell at him, "You no-good bum.

Why do you always hurt your girlfriends?"

Always hurt your girlfriends?

I found my keys, got in my car, and took off.

I never really really loved Luke. I was just in love with

the idea of being in love. Having a boyfriend is what I

wanted, no matter that he and I had little — or almost

nothing — in common. That was my mistake. That's why

I had overlooked the many things about Luke that had

bothered me before he bruised my forearms.

As my bruises faded, I knew I'd never do that again. I

would call it quits the very first time a guy did something

that bothered me, or hurt me — not the last.

Kate learned her lesson the hard way. Now she wants to make sure you don't make the same mistake. Stay away from Bad Boys, period.

Could You Be a Bad-Boy Magnet?

1 The boy you just met has a bunch of close friends. You and the boy have been hanging out a lot recently. But his friends have started calling you and threatening you because they say you're taking up too much of the boy's time. You . . .

    a. Stop answering the phone, get rid of your IM screen name, and change your routine so they don't know when you'll be around. Now they can't call you anymore.

    b. Do exactly what the boy's friends tell you. You talk to the boy only once a week for two minutes and not a sec longer.

    c. Threaten them right back, and then track them down. You aren't scared, even if they are in a gang. You're tougher than they are.

    d. Stop talking to the boy immediately, and tell your parents and the school principal.

I was seeing this guy for three weeks when all of a sudden his friend called to break up with me for him. He was too cowardly to call me himself. —Janelle, 17

2 You have an insanely strong crush on a boy who's known to be angry all the time and who gets into fistfights. But you feel so passionate about this boy, you are crushing on him so hard, it affects your everyday routine. You . . .

a. Suffer in total misery and silence because he's a Bad Boy and you should stay away. You shed buckets of tears and shred plenty of damp tissues and feel really bummed every day.

b. Call your best buds together and enlist them as your Crush Support Group. They'll monitor you so you won't do anything too stupid.

c. Take a boxing class and practice looking angry. Before long, your fighting talents will match your crush's, and you'll make a great couple.

d. Keep repeating to yourself, "This is just a crush on a dud. It will pass in a few weeks." You get involved in a physical activity that's always interested you and keep busy with other things to take your mind off him.

I crushed on this one guy who was, like, so neurotic. He was always trying to find something to get mad about. Whew, did I ditch him fast—what a relief. —Avery, 16

 3 It's springtime. You feel flirtatious and start flirting with the biggest punk in your grade. All your friends and your mom say you should quit trying to get him to notice you. You . . .

a. Swear off boys for the rest of your life because you feel so clueless about them. From now on, you'll confine any thoughts of possible romance to reading romance novels and crying during *Romeo and Juliet.*

b. Stop being so obvious about your flirting. No more standing by his locker. From now on, you'll just e-flirt with him over IMs. What your buds and folks can't see won't hurt them.

c. Can't understand why everybody keeps trying you stop you from having a boyfriend. Your friends are all just jealous, so you're going to give them more to be jealous about. You ask the kid for his posse's cell numbers, and then text them all, too.

d. Listen to your friends and your mom and take a closer look at the boy. He may be cute with those bright blue eyes, but he never goes to class and he did get suspended for stealing out of people's lockers last year. Your mom and friends care about you; they must be right.

 A boy you have a total crush on has terrible mood swings. One day, he talks to you a lot and acts like he's really interested. The next day, he seems very distant and just nods distractedly. Yesterday, he blew past you in the hall with all his boys, without so much as a wave. You . . .

a. Judge it hour by hour, see what kind of day he's having, and react accordingly. If he's in a bad mood, you feel mighty blue too.

b. Send out your best buds to scout in advance what kind of mood he might be in. If it's bad, you buy him candy, give him pep talks, and do your best to cheer him up.

c. Put your whole life on hold and decide to help this boy overcome his severe case of GMS—the Guy Mood Syndrome. Your grades slide, and you never see your fab friends, but you'll do anything to rescue this broody guy.

d. Figure that this boy is moody, but know that you won't tolerate anyone's being disrespectful toward you. So you tell him that he doesn't have to talk to you and you don't have to talk to him. That's the end of that.

Now it's time to find out your true Crush Quotient, your CQ. Tally your answers and find the description that best fits you. If you have a mixture, look at all the breakdowns. Obviously, there's a bit of everything in you, which is fab. Now, can you work on having a little less of the answer A attitude and a little more of the answer D attitude?

Mostly A's: Softie Sophie

Your soft and kind heart is wonderful, but that's not all that makes you special. Look in the mirror. There are strong bones underneath your skin and muscles. So stop being spineless, show some strength, and face whatever guy trials may arise with courage and confidence.

Mostly B's: Edgy Edie

No need to bite your nails all the time. You are a strong girl deep down and you can tell a Bad Boy to back off anytime you want. Sure, it's fun to have crushes and be crushed on, but there's no need to waste your time on Frogs.

Mostly C's: Fighting Fiona

What spirit; what power! You're something to watch. Only one catch—you come on too headstrong every time. If a boy is a Bad Boy, you need to steer clear, even if he pays you the most attention. Don't adopt his bad habits just to please him. You're better than that!

Mostly D's: Just-Right Juliet

You know when to have fun and when to get your work done. You have some fab friends and best buds, and all of you are independent minded and focused on a successful future. You know what boys to steer clear of.

BAD-BOY FACTORS:
What Should You Know about the Bad Boy?

There aren't very many Bad Boys around but each one of them has the potential to hurt you or your girlfriends. So, if you even suspect a boy of being a Bad Boy, steer clear of him and warn your buds as well.

If you won the lottery and could buy any car you want, would you settle for a wrecked and broken-down clunker needing tons of work? Same with guys—why pick a rotten one when others are so nice? —Demitria, 15

There are so many nice boys who try and do a good job every day. Accept the fact that you feel sorry for the Bad Boy, just like you feel sorry for an injured kitten or a bird with a broken wing. Bad Buys have been hurt, for sure. They live sad lives. Some even feel like they have an emptiness they want to fill with beer, pills, or criminal activities. They want to take something to ease their pain, but in the process they may take things from you—your money, your time, your self-esteem.

Know that the Bad Boys can be helped, but *not by you*. That's why schools have caring teachers, hard-working administrators, and dedicated counselors and psychologists. Let any trusted adult know about a Bad Boy if you suspect your friend is involved with one, or worse yet if you make a mistake and become involved with this type of Frog. It's OK to make mistakes—no one will be mad at you for it if you reverse that mistake and ditch the Bad Boy!

BAD BOY FIZZLERS:
What You Should Do about the Bad Boy?

Be a real friend to any Bad Boy from a distance: Direct him to someone who can help him, or mention his name to the right adults. Or, you can even write an anonymous note. Think of the Bad Boy as you would of a brother who's in trouble. You wouldn't just stand by and watch him hurt other girls or self-destruct, would you?

> If you hear about a friend of yours getting hurt by a Bad Boy, do <u>something</u>. Start by telling your mom. —Crystal, 14

Never allow a way critical guy to spew his criticisms all over you like a baby with an upset stomach. Any time a boy says something mean to you, ask yourself why. Is he helpfully trying to improve your form when you lift those five-pound dumbbells during your workouts? Or is he just trying to put you down for no reason?

You spend a lot of time with a Bad Boy, you're gonna feel bad. It's like a contagious disease. —Kay, 15

Whenever you see a hottie who's bad news, immediately think about a beautiful gift you'd get for your b-day. When you open the lovely expensive box, a poisonous snake strikes out. Bad Buys are boys of prey, like we said. The boys of prey target girls who they think are weak and meek, and then they either do mean things to them or become a bad influence on them.

I'd never gotten in trouble before, but then this one dude started talking to me, told me to skip class and hang out with him behind the gym. That spelled trouble, so I got rid of him, fast. —Tania, 13

Bad Boys get a kick out of nice girls suddenly doing something wrong. But they hardly ever show an interest in girls who know what they want, in girls who are strong and independent minded. Set high goals and go after them. That'll keep you hopping and way too busy to spend time with any boys who could be a bad influence. It's really simple—just dis the negative boys around you.

You hang with thugs, you get to be a thug girl. That what you want? No way! —Ladrian, 15

Always know that *you're* in charge, girl. You choose the types of boys to associate with.

The path ahead of you is wonderful, if you make good choices. Make nothing but good ones.

BOY STORY—A Real-Life Story from a Girl Like You

I was seeing this guy who was two years older than I was. We were like *friend* friends for almost two years, and I thought things were great between us. Only problem was that none of my buds and no one in my family liked him at all—especially my sister. She was always telling me how much she hated him, and she was constantly telling me that he wasn't a good guy. But I didn't listen to any of them.

I really didn't understand why they didn't think he was great. I thought he was really good to me and took good care of me. On the other hand, *his* family absolutely *loved* me. His parents always invited me to do things with their relatives.

Eventually Norris and I got very close and we started doing things that I'm not proud of now, things we shouldn't have done. I'm too ashamed to spell them out, but I can say that I only did them because Norris pushed me. He said, "If you love me, you got to do this, or else. . . ." He told me to try this, drink this, smoke that. Never mind my folks. What do they know?

Anyway, my parents ended up finding out about the things we had done, and I got into a lot of trouble. See, what I did was totally against what my family and I believed. My parents told me that I wouldn't be allowed to see Norris ever again. I was so mad at them, because I loved him. I saw him at school, but we weren't allowed to talk on the phone, text message, e-mail, IM, or have any other type of communication.

My parents and I worked out a deal where in six months they'd reconsider if I'd be able to start dating Norris again. Oh, that gave Norris and me some hope. We promised to wait that long and longer, if we had to.

The six months were so hard, and I eagerly counted down the time. I gave up all my outside interests and fab friends, studied hard, stayed home evenings and weekends, and devoted myself to gaining my parents' trust back. My days were tough and long but filled with growing excitement. After six months, my parents asked me to wait another month before seeing Norris. I was crushed but accepted their verdict. What bothered me most was that Norris didn't seem upset when he heard. Then I found out why. While I'd been staying home and hitting the books, he'd been going out and hitting on other girls. He'd pushed them to do bad stuff like he pushed me. He even made a move on my sister!

Norris probably never even meant to wait for me in the first place. All he wanted to do was boss girls around, making them do or get into stuff that was wrong, then move on to the next bunch of naive chicks.

I was in shock over the way things turned out. But I was even more surprised when Norris told me that everything was *my fault*, that I should have done a better job of changing my parents' mind, that he went for the other girls only because I refused to see him. He even said only a dumb fool would wait *that* long! I explained to him that none of it was my fault, told him I thought he was a bigger person than he evidently was, and that he had let me down big-time by lying to me.

At the end of all that waiting, when I needed him most, he didn't care, and really he never had.

I thought I wouldn't be able to pull myself together, but thank goodness I had some amazing friends who helped me. My girl-friends overlooked all those months I'd neglected them, and now they were by my side, letting me cry on their shoulders.

I should've listened to what everybody I cared about was saying about Norris. I never should have let him talk, threaten, or bully me into doing what I knew was wrong! Everyone else saw the *real* Norris. I only saw the shiny surface and flashy smile.

Last week, Norris called me and begged me to see him. He said he wanted to take me out to dinner and give me a gift. He said he'd realized his huge mistake and wanted another chance. What did I tell him? Just one short word, loud and clear: *No!*

Heather, 16

An **A** for you, Heather! You kept your agreement with your parents, you were strong and brave for a long time, and in the end you were empowered enough to say no.

You know what? It's weird, but my mom actually knows a lot about guys. —Nila, 14

The reason Heather didn't get an **A+**, however, is that she refused to listen to her parents, sister, and friends, who sensed or knew that Norris was a bad guy. So from now on, she should believe her friends and especially her parents.

Whenever I meet a new guy and my mom likes him, that's a sure sign he's a keeper. —Monica, 17

Fortunately Heather wised up in the end. Now she knows that promises mean nothing to a Bad Boy. He uses them like Kleenex, to wipe something, to swipe at something. Actually a Bad Boy doesn't even know the meaning of the word *trust*. To him, a promise is just a quick permission slip into your heart.

PRINCESS PROMOTERS: Time for Some Cheerful Add-Justments

What's absolutely fab is that you, either by yourself or with the help of your friends, can disarm any Bad Boy on your radar screen. It's very easy and it just involves you being your happy, cheerful self.

I keep telling myself, combat the bad guys by doing good. —Jill, 15

1. Affection means a kind and tender feeling, a loving spirit toward another. You're a super girl, so now use your kind feelings to offset any unkind feelings some Bad Boys have been spreading around your school. Often just a few Bad Boys can spoil the whole atmosphere of any environment.

    There are these three guys in my school who cause nothing but trouble. Wouldn't be that bad, if they didn't always get my best friend involved in their mess. —Kirby, 14

    You and your friends can reverse this trend of a few Bad Boys hurting a girl. Just get together once a week at lunch and brainstorm about how you can make your school a friendlier, nicer place. What can you do so that not a single girl ever feels she has no one to turn to?

2. Ask the Guidance Department to put out a leaflet you'll write. Its overriding message will be, *Strong girls are hurt less often by the not-nice guys. So be strong.* That way, you'll help all the girls in your world to try and become stronger.

3. You also can start a support group through the Guidance Department, for girls who need to hear about the good and bad guys out there. You, being the smart and stylish girl that you are, can be the one to open their eyes in a kind way, a loving way. Invite girls from other schools to join in your affection connection. Let them in on the secrets you're in on, and show that you're the leaders, the doers, and the advancers.

Boy Secrets

No boy is bad through and through from birth. Some boys haven't had the right kind of home and parenting, others have been neglected and abused, and still others have never been loved by anyone. So these eventual Bad Boys don't know how to act lovingly, but they do know how to act pushy and forceful and super controlling.

> I always try and see how much I can get away with, with anyone, especially with girls. —Eric, 16

Some boys have never been able to believe in anyone. They were promised things as a child, but the promises were broken. Or they've been lied to outright, over and over. As a result, these boys grew up feeling powerless. They try to overcome that feeling by taking over other people's lives.

> Wanna know a secret? Makes me feel powerful to push a girl around. I can always apologize, then do it again. —Raj, 15

When a boy grows up without role models, and he never gets what he really wants—some adult to care for him—he develops strange ideas about what love is.

> I'm only doing it to teach her right. So many chicks are just flat-out weak and need to be taught a lesson. —Kent, 17

To that, we say, *Stop it!* **No boy has the right to hurt a girl, ever.**

Boy File

Take a few file cards and head them up "Bad Boys." Then, using the Crush Code, list all the Bad Boys you know. What makes them bad? Also jot down what you know about some other girls being hurt by them. Then, it's on to you. Have you ever been belittled or criticized by a boy? If so, remember what that critical statement was, and write it down. Then, rewrite the criticism as a positive. If a boy once said to you, "Get out of my way, you dumb cow!" totally rewrite the statement positively, to read, "Kindly step aside, you brilliant gazelle."

You get the idea here, don't you? It's to take any negative or nasty thing any boy ever said in an angry tone of voice or in an ugly teasing manner and rewrite it so it sounds very kind and pleasing and, yes—even funny—to you.

While you cannot reform the actual Bad Boys, you can definitely reform the bogus boys of your past—in your mind. That will help you file them away and it will get the word out that strong and independent-minded girls like you cannot be hurt by any boys of prey.

So whenever you meet a new boy from now on, first thing you do is write his name down on a card using the Crush Code, then put a question mark next to his name. And under that, write whatever comes to your mind about this boy. Then look at your list of phrases and words. Are these words like *nice, friendly, helpful, means what he says*? Or are these words like *grumpy, uses bad language, complains a lot, hates this and that*? If what you observe about this boy is mostly positive, fine. If this is not the case, this is not the boy for you!

Final Exam

So how does the Bad Boy stack up? Take a look at page 33 in Chapter 3 for the report card breakdown info.

The Bad Boy's Report Card

Looks: **P**, though not always
Schoolwork: **F**, usually
Attitude: **F** minus minus
Behavior: **F** minus minus minus
Activities: **F**, though not always

Added up, that means the Bad Boy gets 4 or 5 **F**'s. That puts his Prince-for-you potential at *pitiful*. You know to stay away from the Bad Boys. Warn your friends about them. Bad Boys can do a lot of harm. But strong, powerful, and charging-ahead girls like you can disarm them every time.

PART IV

How to Find Nothing but the Best Crushes, Flirts, and Friend Friends

Boys are way great to know and study with and spend time with, but not if they're a bad influence on you. That means you have to be careful and take it slow in dealing with boys until you know for sure they're good guys.

> *Never get too friendly too fast, and don't sit on a boy's lap in school—it's just not cool.* —Esther, 14

And even with the good guys, it's best always to act with smarts and style. And take pride in yourself. If you don't respect yourself, you might attract boys who don't respect you.

CHAPTER 9

Onward and Upward, Princess!

*n*ow you know: A Prince is a boy whom you feel good being around, and a Frog is a boy who makes you wince like you're uncomfortable, unhappy, or like you just want to run away. You also know that if a boy makes you uncomfortable in any way:

- ❀ Always listen to your heart.
- ❀ Honor your feelings and admit this boy just isn't right for you.
- ❀ *Immediately* stop communicating with this boy.

And you know that the good guys far outnumber the bad guys! Also remember, every time you log off from a Frog, you get stronger. And every time you spend time with a Prince, you win.

Super Self-Esteem Ahead, Princess

Now you know what to do—just separate the Frogs from the Princes. This won't be the easiest thing to do, but you can do it as long as you keep consulting your Boy File and using this book!

You're not going to be fooled. You know to look beneath the surface. Whenever a boy catches your eye, you know how to look more closely. You aren't blinded by smooth talking or his amazing smile.

Garrett is a Prince. He's just about to graduate and go off to college. He and his friends have had lots of crush experience and they've learned from it. Here's what he has to say about finding a cool Prince to spend your time with, and then maybe even making that Prince into a *friend* friend:

1. Go lots of places and events and talk to people.
2. Once you have your eye on a boy and you know he's a Prince, figure out how his personality is.
3. Get to know him better by becoming friends with him.
4. Hang out with him a little more.
5. If you're into each other, make it known and start going out with him.

Sure you'll find the right guy, if you want to. Trust me.
—Garrett, 18

Solo Flight, Soul Flight

It's *your choice* whether you want to include boys as you go through school. Nobody says you have to invite them along on your fab journey!

Me and my friends have a blast most every day.
All of us have major crushes at the moment, which
makes our times even better 'cause
we have a gazillion things
to dish about.
— Jennifer, 14

Yes, nice boys can add a lot of laughs to your life during these wonderful years. But boys aren't necessary for you to be the best girl you can be. You can pick and choose from all the nice guys around—those who are crush-worthy, flirt-worthy, or *friend* friend–worthy. Just skip over boys who don't measure up. Remember that you are not somebody's medic or mom or mind-fixer. You have your own mind, soul, and body to tend to. You're busy with your own wonderful and productive life!

I enjoy being single 'cause the last guy <u>friend</u> friend I had made my life, like, pretty bad for a while. —Leila, 16

Getting attached too early to any kind of boy, no matter how super he is, can really slow you down. So it's most important that you are proud of who you are right *now*—a unique and magnificent young lady—with all the possibilities this wonderful world holds right ahead of you. You are that bright mega star of the now and the future that lights up the world for all of us.

My top secret: Being single is totally terrif'. You can do what you feel like. Nobody ever tells you what to do and what not to do. —Jeanne, 16

Being without a boyfriend is fabulous. It frees you to focus on the main thing: Yourself!

PRINCESS PROMOTERS:
Final Add-Justment

The last add-justment you must make is simple: This is the *Aah*-add-justment. What do you like? What makes you truly happy? When are you happiest? Is it when you listen to a hot song, flip through a hip mag, or IM with your buds? Is it when you chill in front of the TV or flop on your bed and take a nap or sit in front of the mirror and try a new 'do or a new you?

1. Make an *Aah*-list of things you just *love* to do, try, shop for.
2. Make another *Aah*-list of your favorite and sweetest friends.
3. And now make a list of boys who have Princely potential.

Isn't it exciting just to think about all this? Sure it is. It's all about what you want. It's all in your power.

Here is a quick checklist to remind you of your new relationship powers. This Crushes, Flirts, and *Friend* Friends Final is a fun exam.

The Crushes, Flirts, and Friend Friends Final

Directions: Check next to those items you feel very confident about. Each check is worth 10 points.

1. _____ Can you define what a crush is?

2. _____ Do you know what's okay in flirting and what's not?

3. _____ Do you know what having a *friend* friend means?

4. _____ Do you know the difference between a Frog and a Prince?

5. _____ Can you identify the Geeks in your school?

6. _____ Do you know how to recognize and befriend a Go-getter?

7. _____ Do you know what qualities make a Prince so special?

8. _____ Can you recognize the Flunkies at your school?

9. _____ Can you identify the Toadies?

10. _____ Can you spot and avoid the Bad Boys?

APPENDIX

Cool Crush-Smart Chick Tools

This section offers a selection of the latest and coolest print materials plus Internet resources specifically designed to lend you a hand as you make lots more friends.

TEEN 'ZINES

CosmoGIRL!
224 West 57th Street
New York, NY 10019
www.cosmogirl.com

Girls' Life Magazine
4517 Hartford Road
Baltimore, MD 21214
www.girlslife.com

Seventeen Magazine
1440 Broadway
13th floor
New York, NY 10017-5514
www.seventeen.com

Teen People
P.O. Box 999
Radio City Station
New York, NY 10101
www.teenpeople.com

Teen Vogue
Conde Nast
4 Times Square
New York, NY 10013
www.teenvogue.com

YM
G&J USA Publishing
375 Lexington Avenue
New York, NY 10018
www.ym.com

TEEN BOOKS

The Boyfriend Clinic: The Final Word on Flirting, Dating, Guys, and Love (Seventeen) by Melanie Mannarino, Sagebrush, 2000.

The Frog Buster: A Girl's Guide for Survival in the Dating Swamp by Klayne I. Rasmussen et al., IntraLife, 2002.

The Girls' Guide to Guys: Straight Talk for Teens on Flirting, Dating, Breaking Up, Making Up & Finding True Love by Julie Taylor, Three Rivers Press, 2000.

A Smart Girl's Guide to Boys: Surviving Crushes, Staying True to Yourself & Other Stuff (American Girl Library Series) by Nancy Holyoke and Bonnie Timmons, American Girl, 2001.

Teen Love: On Relationships, A Book for Teenagers by Kimberly Kirberger, HCI, 1999.

FRIENDLY CHICK SITES

www.freshangles.com—A teen e-zine.

www.cyberteens.com—A site with several areas of interest.

http://education.indiana.edu/cas/adol/adol.html—Adolescence Directory On-Line, a service of Indiana University. Has many links to other sites.

Yahoo.com's links to teen e-zines. This list has pretty much something for every interest.

www.gurl.com—Gurl.com has many areas of interest for teenage girls.

Also Available
by Erika V. Shearin Karres, Ed.D.

Mean Chicks, Cliques, and Dirty Tricks

As Featured in

Teen People!

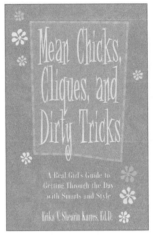

Trade Paperback
$8.95, ISBN: 1-58062-933-4

Fab Friends and Best Buds

Trade Paperback
$8.95, ISBN: 1-59337-293-0